Artists Handbooks
Art in Public
what, why and how

edited by
Susan Jones

AN Publications

By giving access to information, advice and debate, AN Publications aims to:

- empower artists individually and collectively to strengthen their professional position
- raise awareness of the diversity of visual arts practice and encourage an equality of opportunity
- to stimulate good working practices throughout the visual arts.

Credits

Picture research, captions, examples, Further reading, Contacts & Developing skills	Susan Jones
Index	Susanne Atkin
Proof reader	Heather Cawte Winskell (100 Proof)
Cover illustration	Helen Chadwick (see page 3)
Design & Layout	Neil Southern
Printed	Mayfair Printers, Print House, William Street, Sunderland, SR1 1UI
Grant aid	AN Publications gratefully acknowledges financial support from the Arts Council
Copyright	The writers, photographers and Artic Producers Publishing Co Ltd © 1992

ISBN 0 907730 18 3

AN Publications is an imprint of
Artic Producers Publishing Co Ltd
PO Box 23, Sunderland SR4 6DG tel 091 567 3589

Acknowledgements

All well as the writers for this book, AN Publications thanks Barbara Taylor, Jayne Earnscliffe and Philippa Goodall and Kate Green of Photo Call for their specialist research, and also Antonia Payne, Hilary Gresty, Panchayat, Ian Rashid, David Kaye, Malcolm Miles, Barclay Price, Simon Fenoulhet, Loraine Leeson, Sandy Nairne, Projects Environment and the many others who contributed information for the writers.

We are indebted, as ever, not only to the many artists who responded so fully to a survey we conducted as part of the book's research but to all artists and others who contributed information, photographs and their enthusiasm to this book.

Last but not least, thanks are given to Colin Wilbourn, Ged McCormack, Fran Bugg, Pat Smith and Barrie Ormsby who formed the advisory group which began planning this book in 1990, and to the hardworking team at AN Publications who make books like this a reality.

Cover
Detail from *Wreath to Pleasure* by **Helen Chadwick**, who used fifteen hundred tulips, engine oil and a plum for this commission to construct a still-life photograph for the BBC Billboard Art Project in 1992. "I wanted to make a very intimate image extremely public, an image that was provocative in some way but which you would not expect to see on a billboard." Photo: the artist.

Contents

- Foreword 6

- Introduction 7

1 • Art in public 11
Government 12, Arts frameworks 15, Conflicts & dilemmas 17

2 • Roles & functions 28
Specific 28, Artists 29, Installation 29, Engagement 31, Language 33, Integration 37, Temporary 38, Mediation 41

3 • Attributes & attitudes 44
Crucial qualities 44, Changing attitudes 45, Production 46, Organisation 47, Persistence 47, Developing skills 48, Environment 48, Integration 48, Work with planners 53, Time-scale 53, Collaboration 57, Flexibility 57, Teams 59

4 • Approaches 63
Agencies 63, Visual artists 64, Enhancement 65, American models 66, Approaches 67, Local solution 70, Wider context 71, Categories 74, Artists' interests 77

5 • Applications & proposals 78
Commission structures 79, Artists as initiators 79, Open competitions 81, Planned development 83, Preparation 84, Principles 85, Quality control 86, What is a proposal? 89, Supporting material 90, Visual material 91, Portfolio 91, Making designs work 91, What is a brief? 94, Get it in writing 97, Rejection or success 97

6 • Working methods 99
Subversion 99, Blurring distinctions 100, Transient Works 101, Reservations 102, Invisible collaborations 103, Creating teams 105, Art for the non-art venture 109, Community 109, Strengths & issues 111

7 • **Presentation 112**
Registers & indexes 112, Springboard 116, Empowerment 116,
Responses to a brief 119, Interviews 120, Launch 124

8 • **Developing the artwork 127**
First encounters 127, Consultant/artist 131, Artist/consultant 133,
Negotiation 139, Consultation 140, Reaching people 142, Attractions
144

9 • **Further reading 145**
Publications 145, Articles & magazines 148

10 • **Contacts 151**
Art & environment 151, Artist-led groups 152, Artists' registers 153,
Art councils and boards 154, Information services 154, Professional
bodies 155, Public art agencies 155, Sculpture trusts 155

11 • **Developing skills 156**
MA courses 156, Degree courses 156

12 • **Contributors 157**

13 • **Index 159**

Examples

• **Developing skills 48**

• **Time-scale 53**

• **Working with industry 61**

• **Developing a private commission 82**

• **Responding to a brief 87**

• **Example of a brief 92**

• **Artist's initiative 108**

• **Making slides 113**

• **Making an application 129**

• **Artist/consultant 132,**

• **Developing a project 134**

• **Siting a commission 138**

Foreword

Conrad Atkinson
Chair of Fine Art,
University of
California, USA
The relationship between public and private is a key factor in contemporary discussions about art and art practice. The debate which has been crudely posed on one hand as "Out of the galleries and into the streets" in 1968 (later twisted out of shape and turned around to "Out of the streets into the galleries") and on the other as "art for the masses" has received infinite refinement over the past two decades.

The debate has been interestingly revealing about the relationship between artists and what would have at one time been called 'the State' – a concept increasingly blurred by three factors. Firstly by the great upheavals in the East, secondly by the global characteristics of consumption and consumerism, and thirdly by the sense of the latter's nemesis in the growing awareness of finite resources and a crisis in ecology.

This shifting relationship between public and private is evident in the topsy-turvy world of arts in Russia where the official now seems to be unofficial and the avant-garde the official.

In many ways, the rich dialogue about the context for art in public places is an attempt to fill the space in the West left by the collapse of the avant-garde.

Clearly, the meanings produced by the built environment are crucial to the quality of life, and the complexity of discourse implies a package of notions and shifting ideas which form some of the questions raised so intelligently by this book.

Introduction

This book, published at a time when debate and controversy about the purpose and value of art in public is raging, takes the broadest view of the context and practicalities of current visual arts practice taking place in public settings. Covering permanent and temporary works from sculpture to holography and from decorative paving to copy-art, it shows how artists have responded to sites ranging from a tower block to a corporate headquarters and from schools to country footpaths, sites which vary enormously in terms of nature, usage and public expectation.

This is not another book extolling the virtues of 'public art'. Using these words would have defined the content too narrowly, because this term has come to describe a particular type of work in a particular type of setting: generally permanent and usually architecturally defined art and craft works sited in city centres or urban post-industrial locations undergoing major revitalisation.

Much of such work has been generated through the energies of the public art agencies who argue that public art is "the key to the rediscovery of the public domain upon which the survival of our cities depend... one of the building blocks of urban regeneration." Questioning the role of those agencies though, Artangel Trust's John Carson said "The work of public art agencies in Britain might be correctly characterised as being concerned with grand personal artistic statements lending themselves to corporate plaza prestige (and) competitive artistic circuses such as garden festivals...."

Public Art Forum membership leaflet

'An Introduction to Common Ground' *Public Art Review,* Spring/ Summer, 1991

Without doubt, public art agencies have generated new sources of income for the visual arts and enabled some artists to gain a high profile through involvement with major civic schemes. But Edna Read, formerly Director of City Gallery Arts Trust, questioned whether the growth in the number of career art administrators has done anything to raise the profile of artists: "Is it anything to do with the difference between the way in which writers' successful promotion by an agent feeds the agent, whereas most arts administrators are salaried and their relationship with artists is far less well-defined."

Letter in *Artists Newsletter,* October, 1992

Introduction

In this book, the artist/agent relationship is discussed, and although one writer makes an analogy between public art agencies and estate agents: "they keep seller and buyer apart... as their fee is charged on the selling price, it is in their interest to get the best possible price", another argues they perform "a valuable role, speaking for and negotiating on behalf of artists who are not that assertive".

In this country, because art in public has developed outwith the mainstream gallery and curator system, there is a gulf between it and other kinds of visual arts. This is exacerbated by the lack of critical writing about commissioned works: although exhibitions are reviewed, art in other kinds of public setting is rarely mentioned, other than in terms of who commissioned or sponsored it and how proud they are of it. Some artists complain privately of the stigma of being called a 'public artist'. Not all the art world is even convinced that putting art in public places is a good idea though, Tim Hilton having recently argued "Art is best served by getting people into galleries, not by spilling artists all over the place."

Another burning issue at the forefront of the debate concerns 'the public': who are they, what are their expectations, are they consulted or involved in the making of works which will infringe on their lives, and are their needs and expectations met by the resulting artworks? Art historian Jonathan Harris, in response to an article on Richard Serra's sculpture maintained that "Public art, like architecture, is the economic and intellectual property of a set of professional élites (planners, producers, critics), whose use of public resources generally has no recourse to any kind of democratic process." This is endorsed by David Baggaley who wrote "Art which places itself outside its more usual contexts in the search for new audiences will have to pay considerably more attention to the conditions of public meaning than has previously been the case."

In 1991, the Arts Council put into action its campaign to encourage local government and others to allocate a percentage of building budgets to the commission of art or craft. By publishing *Percent for Art: a review*, they intended to prove the argument by showing the successful results of such policies in America and elsewhere.

But there are major differences in the way artists and other design professionals are regarded in the UK and in other countries, and for percent for art to work here, traditional attitudes about status, roles and responsibilities will have to change. Robert Holden, reporting on the Landscape Institute's 1991 symposium pointed to one of the differences. "In France architects and artists mix; indeed architects *are* artists. Artists don't mix in at the Royal Institute of British Architects, and architectural education has been hived off into the realm of science. Similarly, art education focuses too often on the end goal of the gallery system."

'Platform for the voices of despair', *The Guardian*, October 6, 1992

The Guardian, September 26, 1992

'Politics, patronage & public art', *Circa* 54, 1990

'Irish Stew' *Building Design*, May 3, 1991

This was also articulated by Deyan Sudjic as "A neurotic climate of mutual incomprehension and suspicion between art and architecture... No architect worth their salt can bear to allow an artist the space in a building that matters to them to make their mark. ... And the closer they come to each other's territory, the more tense and difficult the relationship becomes." Unless responsibility for professional indemnity – financial guarantee for the quality of work – can be shared amongst all involved in a collaborative scheme, there will continue to be a natural reticence amongst architects to accepting artists as equal partners.

Furthermore, Andrew Guest, Director of the Scottish Sculpture Trust, described percent for art as merely a tool, as capable of leading to the "perpetuation and further entrenchment of a limited perception of the role of art in society, depriving artists and public of a fuller participation in art" as it is of challenging the status quo.

And what of the quality of artworks themselves? Ian Robb, artist and lecturer at Duncan of Jordanstone College of Art has voiced his concern about the danger of "being swamped by low-cost art litter." Critic Peter Dormer's view is that "Most public art objects fail because they tend not to be very interesting; they do not capture the imagination because they have less wit, meaning and interest than a cleverly designed and well-executed 45-second lager advertisement on television." Artist Tess Jaray – whose own work hasn't been compromised by the transition from paint to bricks as a medium to create a dialogue between artwork and recipient – has also commented that "As with architecture, some public art is downright naff."

It is impossible, however, to list in abstract the factors which, if satisfied, will determine whether an art work in a public setting will be well regarded by the people who have to experience it every day. Similarly, an architect's notion of what constitutes appropriate housing can only be proved if people move in and enjoy living there. There are arguments to support the low-key, common sense approach, one encapsulated by Common Ground's way of commissioning artworks which "should have meaning for the present-day inhabitants and for future generations, and become part of the life of the community", an approach highlighting their concern not to alienate any of their audience.

How people receive and respond to art works in public sites is often only heard about if they are vandalised or provoke public outcry. But often damage is done not because it is a work of art, rather because is it something accessible which encroaches on an environment. People feel no more need to be reverential about an art work than they do about buildings, advertising hoardings and fencing.

Richard Deacon said he wanted to make sculpture "that interferes with the space... I'm not interested in making a play park and I'm not

'Shaping up for a war of works', *The Guardian*, October 8, 1992

'The Cream of Philadelphia', *Artists Newsletter,* December 1992

Context & Collaboration, report of the International Public Art Symposium, 1990

'Lipstick on the face of a gorilla', *The Independent,* September 9, 1992

'Lobby puts weight behind public art', *Building Design*, April 10, 1992

Joanna Morland, Common Ground

Introduction

Art Monthly, October, 1992 interested in making a subservient sculpture, but neither am I interested in making a dominant or aggressive thing.... I've got no objection to people sitting on the work, but I don't want it to become a bench." The people sitting on it, however, may nevertheless perceive it as a bench and treat is as such, dropping litter around it or inscribing their names or those of their favourite football teams on it. Richard Serra's works have suffered from such interpretation, for whatever his intention for them, they have been perceived by homeless people as shelters and outdoor toilets. Andy Goldsworthy's view is that the public have to be respected:

Aspects 32, Spring, 1986 "Although my work is intensely personal, it is usually made in a public place and has always had to accept other people's use of it, whether that be enjoyable, restrictive, aggravating or destructive."

Reported in *Art within Reach* Problems with the reception of art in public are often blamed on bad mediation. Antony Gormley believed his sculpture *Two Stones* sited at Singleton Village School, Kent was vandalised "because it was just plonked onto the building site and no attempt made to introduce it to the local community." The assumption is that mediation isn't the artist's job, but someone else's, a view endorsed by Patricia Bickers, editor of *Art Monthly* who said on Radio 4's Kaleidoscope that "Art does not create a place for itself... it is magazines, curators, writers who do that."

In looking for models for how art in public might be developed here in the future, examples from other European countries and from North America are often cited. But public art is a mainstream activity there, artists collaborating on equal terms, curating exhibitions, initiating their own commissions and setting their own agendas. The UK could only adopt such models if its traditionally paternalistic attitude to artists gave way to recognising the value of direct contact between clients and other design professionals. Lee Corner comments in this book that "Ideally, an agency acts as a buffer against fundraising problems, multiple agendas and intransigent commissioners. However, it is also a buffer to direct dialogue, which for many artists is an adrenalin source for new ideas and creative solutions."

Successful relationships and creative solutions – whether collaborations between design professionals or between artists and people – result from taking a long-term approach. Many artist or practice-led projects are committed to this philosophy, enabling the public not to be a passive audience for the art, but a contributor to the body of ideas on which the art concentrates. This method, which can result in the successful enhancement of the visual environment and an improvement of the quality of people's lives in a strategic way, has the added reward of leading to empowerment of artists and other people. It can create mutual respect, raise the status of artists and enable them to present their private and unique experiences as artists to a public space.

1 • Art in public

Sara Selwood Public art is notoriously ill-defined. Until the mid-'80s it was often regarded as synonymous with 'sculpture in the open air', although some critics maintained it took more than an outdoor site to make sculpture public. It can be located in relatively inaccessible places such as offices, schools and hospitals and consequently might be more accurately located in the ideological realm of the 'public sphere'. It can be produced for, and owned by, the community whether or not they actively participate in its creation. It can be considered a 'funding' category since the funding source is likely to be what defines it as art as opposed to street furniture. It can be the product of state intervention, corporate investment, art world guerrillas or even implicated in party politics. It can combine self-conscious avant-gardism and heritage culture; can be parachuted in and site-specific; ephemeral and permanent; time-based and static and more or less environmentally friendly. It can also represent a battleground between the artist's freedom of expression and the public's right to choose.

If its definitions are contradictory, the litany of its merits is relatively constant, especially in respect of the contribution it is supposed to make to urban regeneration. In the *Strategy for Public Art in Cardiff Bay*, the Public Art Consultancy Team rehearsed many of its accepted wisdoms. They described public art as a cultural investment vital to the economic recovery of cities. They credited it with attracting companies, investment and cultural tourism; adding to land values; boosting employment; increasing use of open spaces; reducing vandalism and wear and tear on buildings, humanising the environment; making places safer and encouraging community pride. But the derogatory colloquialisms public art inspires suggest a different story – 'turds on the piazza'; 'parachute art'; 'developers' equine'; 'corporate baubles', 'lipstick on the face of a gorilla'.

Public art flourished during a decade when the government's intention was to decrease public spending on arts and increase their earning power and capacity to attract sponsorship. Public and private

11

sectors often combined forces to invest in public art, even when they both had different aspirations for it. But in the current economic climate, both sectors need to be re-convinced that it is still a worthwhile investment. A University of Westminster survey in 1992 showed that several local authorities are far from confident about their own promotion of public art. They want to know more about its function and the nature of the relationship between cultural and economic regeneration.

Public art necessarily reflects the interests and dynamics of its funding bodies. This chapter reflects on how those relationships work and the kinds of implication they have for the production of public art.

Government

Robert Hutchinson & Peter Wilmott, *Urban Trends 1*, Policy Studies Institute, 1992

"The decay at the heart of Britain's cities is one of the biggest challenges faced by government. Successive administrations have tried to reverse the trends. The aims have been to support and stimulate environmental renewal, to encourage new jobs and give residents a better quality of life and new hope."

In 1977, a Labour Party report *The Arts and the People* proposed that Urban Programme funding could be used to encourage community-based activities and contribute to unified neighbourhoods. Art could help overcome neglect and alienation felt in deprived areas and thereby ultimately prevent much crime and vandalism which it supposed were contingent upon them. This idealistic vision was fully consistent with the then Labour government's policy on inner cities. The White Paper it published the same year, *Policy for the Inner Cities* – which led to the Inner Urban Act 1978 – was the first comprehensive policy statement to acknowledge the inner cities as a definable, cohesive problem. Under Urban Programme, Labour prioritised particular cities and parts of cities needing support for regeneration. It introduced measures premised on the notions of state rather than private investment, social rather than economic improvements, the needs of the community rather than those of the individual.

In the face of soaring unemployment and riots in the early '80s, successive Conservative governments expanded Urban Programme. By 1984/5, they had increased the funds to local government through it by nearly twelvefold. In 1987, the government started channelling much of the funding for priority areas through Urban Development Corporations (UDCs) – local quangos responsible for regeneration of run-down inner city land. Mainstream local authority Urban Programme money was primarily directed to helping new businesses and training. By 1991, total government spending on inner cities exceeded £892 million.

One of government's objectives was to 'pump prime' schemes which would attract private investment or 'partnerships'. By 1992, UDCs were reported to have succeeded in attracting over £10.6 billion in private sector investment with only £1.8 billion of public funding. The sheer scale of state investment in areas of urban deprivation and the incentives offered to the private sector inevitably created opportunities for arts development. This included public art, which the Cabinet Office endorsed in 1988. The concentration of funding in urban areas largely accounts for why public art is considered an urban genre.

In order to be regarded as a legitimate aspect of urban policy, perceptions of the arts had to change. Whereas in the '70s the arts were commonly considered to occupy a separate realm from that of the everyday world, by the '80s, as one of the so-called 'cultural industries' they were administratively and ideologically regarded as grounded in economic 'realities'. Because the arts were perceived as "sustaining employment"

Richard Cole *Windy Nook.*
Photo: Keith Pattison

This 5,500 square metre piece built on a former colliery and slag heap and made from 2,500 tons of stone and recycled pillars, was designed as a walk, play and viewing area. Commissioned by Gateshead Metropolitan Borough Council in 1985 as part of their award-winning public art programme, construction was enabled by Gateshead's Community Programme assisted by MSC.

Ray Smith's **2.5 acre *Red Army*** at Gateshead Garden Festival 1990, sponsored by British Steel, Swan Hunter and International Paints, now in the collection of Lord Palumbo. **Photo:** Northern Arts

"I wanted to fill the site with a work that emphasised its scale, making it seem more vast. I drew some figures with upraised arms and realised the ambiguity in the gesture, variously interpreted as joy or celebration, defiance or terror." (*Festival Landmarks*). At the time it was much vaunted as "the biggest single work in the biggest exhibition of contemporary art in Britain".

This major investment stopped when MSC became the Training Commission and subsequently the Training Agency in 1988. Training was devolved to regional Training and Enterprise Councils in England and Local Enterprise Councils in Scotland.

and "a cost-effective means of job creation", arts-based training for employment attracted considerable government investment. At its peak in 1986/87, the Manpower Services Commission (MSC) Community Programme, funded by the Department of Employment, had generated 6,751 places on 359 'cultural' projects, with the cost of the programme estimated at £24 million. In some regions, MSC projects together with funds channelled through the Department of the Environment, the Home Office, the Department of Trade and Industry (DTI) and the National Health Service provided more by way of arts funding than regional arts associations and local authorities combined.

Public art was especially conspicuous in garden festivals. Initially inspired by a West German post-war scheme to reconstruct bombed cities, their ethos reflected the optimism of the Festival of Britain. Five biennial festivals were funded by the DoE via UDCs, Derelict Land

Grants and Urban Programme. The intention was to stimulate investment in and regeneration of those areas of Britain scarred by the abandonment of manufacturing industries. They reclaimed disused land, secured long-term redevelopment and celebrated urban renewal. In Liverpool in 1984, Stoke in 1986, Glasgow in 1988, Gateshead in 1990 and Ebbw Vale in 1992, millions have been spent removing and camouflaging industrial debris. Art became as much a part of these festivals as horticulture, rides and fast food.

Arts frameworks

Public art has always occupied a strange position in the Arts Council's remit. When it was established in 1946, it inherited the dual objectives of promoting the arts as part of people's daily lives and supporting professional artists. It promptly withdrew from disseminating the arts at the sites of popular culture such as holiday camps, works' canteens, factories, shops and schools and between the mid-'60s and '80s, prioritised "housing the arts" in separate buildings. It wasn't until the '70s and under considerable pressure that the Arts Council made gestures towards the "community" – which its first Chairman Maynard Keynes had patronisingly referred to as "the welfare side."

However, the Arts Council had always promoted sculpture in 'the open air' – in public parks (which were always considered to be the 'natural' location for sculptures to be seen), the landscape, cities and at garden festivals. It never had a funding category for public art as such, but allocated funds to it under various headings – 'Works of Art for Public Buildings' in '77/79, 'Art in Public Sites' in '79/80 and 'Art in Public Places from '85. The visual arts department consistently encouraged both public and private sectors to invest in public art – even to the extent of offering them financial incentives to do so.

By the '80s, its attitude to public art was reflected in the Arts Council's overall policy. Following government calls for private investment in the arts, the council increasingly took to justifying public support of the arts in terms of their economic benefits. This is reflected in the titles of policy documents – The Great British Success Story (1983), Partnerships (1984), Better Business in the Arts (1988). Between 1988 and 1991, at the behest of the Minister for the Arts, the council ran the Incentive Funding Scheme intended to help arts organisations to become more financially enterprising. Public art agencies counted amongst its beneficiaries.

The promotion of public art was also boosted by Arts Council policy to invest in the regions. The Glory of the Garden development strategy proposed a more equitable geographical distribution of its expenditure and the creation of more "centres of excellence". Although targeted at local authorities, the Arts Council also increased the value of its grants to the RAAs. In 1985 for example, it devolved £250,000 to them to assist public art commissions, in the expectation this would yield £3 million of matching funding. Its more recent strategy, 'Arts 2000', is intended to "refurbish the cultural fabric of the nation". It has involved designating different regional cities 'cities of culture'. Public art is sure to feature in the celebrations for 1996, the year of the visual arts to be hosted by the Northern region.

In recent years, Arts Council support of public art has been bound up with the fortunes of the visual arts department. After losing direct responsibility for the Hayward and Serpentine galleries and for exhibition touring, the department moved increasingly towards an advocacy role. In 1988, it effectively ceased funding permanent works of public art directly, although public art initiatives – usually temporary – continue to be resourced under other categories.

In 1988 the Arts Council launched the percent for art campaign, designed to employ the visual arts in urban regeneration. It was targeted at local authorities and UDs, and relied on their motivation to enhance the quality of life for local residents and create focal points for promoting social cohesion. The campaign echoed government policy precisely. Percent for art was intended to "transform the climate for investment while improving the urban environment." By July 1990, the Arts Council estimated having spent £32,000 on encouraging developers to adopt the policy and had committed another £30,000 over the next three years to support the creation of new posts in four local authorities aimed at introducing the percent for art policy within the planning system. The 1992 Arts Council draft policy *Towards a National Arts and Media Strategy* calls for percent for art to be made mandatory.

The Arts Council's second campaign of 1988, *An Urban Renaissance*, was also concerned with increasing public and private sector co-operation. By 1989, it published a report endorsing 16 projects which it claimed had acted as "magnets – attracting people, tourism, businesses and jobs to an area", which had served as "catalysts for regeneration", enhanced "the visual quality of the built environment", provided "a focal point for community pride and identity" and helped "build self-confidence in individuals." Each had been supported by partnerships forged between local authority, agencies of Urban Programme, arts funders or businesses. The current Arts Council/British Gas Awards scheme 'Working for Cities' similarly seeks to demonstrate how the arts "can breathe new life into derelict, neglected or just forgotten areas."

"Percent for art is a... formula rooted in a belief that artists and craftspeople have a distinctive role to play in the design of public space... that reserves a percentage of the estimated cost of any capital work for art or craft... (it) usually results in a commission for an artist or craftsperson to make a work for a public place, but this is not the only option." (*Percent for Art: a Review*)

Tess Jaray's **pavement for Centenary Square Birmingham.** **Photo:** Birmingham City Council, Department of Planning & Architecture

This small-scale pattern in orange, ochre, red and brown rectangular bricks creates a colossal sweep of shade and light and appears to change colour with the position of the sun. Jaray also designed bollards, seats and lamp-posts and was one of seven artists commissioned through Public Art Commissions Agency to make work for Birmingham International Convention Centre and Centenary Square as part of a percent for art policy.

Conflicts & dilemmas

Arts Council & local authorities

The Arts Council's role in promoting art in public has been essentially strategic, particularly its advocacy of projects which attract other sources of income. Plural funding has ideological and pragmatic advantages: it multiplies the benefits of any one investor, and leads to greater diversification in arts provision – considered a strength in a pluralist society. The Arts Council pump-primed percent for art officer posts in the expectation they would become self-supporting or devolve to the appropriate local authorities, and it praised public art agencies for being "hybrids of the public and private sectors."

Arts Council public art policies have been directed primarily at local authorities, even though their ability to invest in public art is necessarily constrained. Although local authority spending on the arts had grown to exceed that of central government, following abolition of the metropolitan counties in 1986, the government imposed limits on their expenditure, especially the "high spending authorities". By the end of the the '80s, authorities were experiencing difficulties with collecting poll tax, charge capping, proposals for compulsory competitive tendering and diminution of education budgets. Since their spending on the arts is purely discretionary, many have had to cut back on their commitments in the areas of arts and recreation.

Consequently, if local authorities decide to commit funds to public art, they are effectively obliged to do so through capital rather than revenue expenditure. And in order to avoid the restrictions imposed on their arts funding, they have to use budgets allocated to planning departments for 'environmental improvements'.

These conditions have inevitably affected the implementation of percent for art. *The Report of the Percent for Art Steering Committee* in 1990 listed 30 local authorities and UDCs in England "understood to have adopted percent for art at committee level in local plans or building policies." The Arts Council's annual report for 1989/90 referred to 50 unnamed local authorities in the UK committed to the principle. But as a survey in 1992 showed, the possession of a percent for art policy is no guarantee of its implementation. In practice, there are very few percent for art schemes in which a percentage of the total cost of developments is allocated to art. The Arts Council's *Percent for art: a review* cites no more than three examples.

Local authorities' promotion of public art consequently employs other strategies, and the majority of local authority public art projects are realised through partnerships. *The Public Art Report* published by Public Art Forum in 1990 confirmed that single local authority departments are rarely sole funders. Funding partners are drawn from the public sector – county and district authorities, RAAs, development corporations and MSC. Many attract small-scale sponsorship from local companies.

The *Report of the Percent for Art Committee* proposed that public art projects would serve to integrate local authority departments across a wide range of interests – environmental, community-based, health, civic and educational activities. It could be argued that such collaborations indicate "a growing understanding for the potential of such work", but they will not necessarily define that potential as 'art'. Many local authorities are in fact loth to fund public art as such, although they may be inclined to spend money on environmental improvements. They may even refer to such improvements as 'art' because their aspirations for the project transcend the norm, because the objects

John Maine's **iron post, Lewisham. Photo:** the artist

A 15-strong Lewisham 2000 team, established to design and build the new town centre, included John Maine who continues to be a consultant, his aim to make the whole town "a work of art". Project Manager Mike Jackson sees him as someone with a different perspective who stimulates others to come up with surprising solutions. "There is a contained intensity about a dense row of Maine's cast iron bollards... they are unequivocally of our time, but not self-consciously so.... The strategy is one of presence and focus, rather than a vain attempt at assertion over the visual cacophony of the High Street." (*The Furnished Landscape*)

produced lend a sense of authenticity to a place or because they display a high degree of craftsmanship or skill – popularly regarded as indicating quality in art.

A major issue raised by local authority involvement with public art is the imposition of aesthetic judgements and notions of artistic quality. As *The Planning Policy Guidance Notes* state: "Aesthetics is an extremely subjective matter. Planning authorities should not impose their tastes on development simply because they believe them to be superior. Developers should not be compelled to conform to the fashion of the moment at the expense of individuality, originality or traditional styles. Nor should they be asked to adopt designs which are unpopular with their customers."

Planners have complained that their professional training fails to give them the skills of confidence to deal with aesthetic matters. Any

Jim Dine, *Venus.* Photo: Broadgate Developments

Sited at 155 Bishopsgate in London's 29-acre Broadgate development, these bronze torsos seem like enormous fragments of antiquity, as though found by an archeologist excavating an ancient palatial building. Works of art by such artists are "enhancing the nature of the environment, providing scale, humanity... that is the fundamental ingredient of successful urban design." (*Art at Broadgate*)

ability they have to uphold artistic standards is likely to be further compromised by the implementation of Compulsory Competitive Tendering. As the research by the University of Westminster revealed, some local authorities need assurances about the public art they promote. Responding to this need is all the more urgent since, given the 'falling off' of private sector development, when many local authorities wish to cast themselves as major promoters of public art. To do so confidently, they need "trained staff, sufficiently well-briefed to make constructive and progressive decisions."

As one of the senior planners at Leicester City Council put it: "Art in the environment, mural painting and street sculpture is not my main concern.... Rather I am interested in ways in which the artist's perception of the environment can help us sharpen our own, better equip us to see potential for improvement."

Corporate sector

The issue of artistic compromise also colours perceptions of the corporate sector's involvement in public art. Not all private developers are convinced of the efficacy of expenditure on public art. Some see percent for art as an unwelcome addition to costs. However, there are those who employ public art to denote the 'quality' of individual developments. In this sense, it may be regarded as a business investment. The fact that works by such prestigious artists as Richard Serra, Jim Dine and George Segal are integrated into Rosehaugh Stanhope's Broadgate development doubtless contributed to attracting major American, European and Japanese companies to locate there.

The government has consistently encouraged the private sector to contribute to the arts, particularly through business sponsorship. But statistics suggest that such support is relatively limited. Although levels fluctuate, during 1990/91 it was estimated that sponsorship accounted for 5% of the overall value of the arts economy, the visual arts receiving 12.5% of such sponsorship funding.

Despite the relatively small-scale of corporate sponsorship, private sector contributions to the arts in the public sphere are still regarded as contentious. When it comes to commissioning, purchasing or other forms of support, corporations implicitly, if not explicitly, suppress or promote a particular aesthetic according to their own taste, or that assumed to be their clients'. The ABSA and 'Working for Cities' awards, and Incentive Funding, may be perceived by corporate funders as endorsing their aesthetic judgement.

There is also much uncertainty as to whether private investment is improving social and economic problems. In his Presidential address to the Royal Town Planning Institute in 1988, Francis Tibbalds described what he perceived as the inevitable consequences of such investment. He feared that London in particular "is drifting towards a '1984-style' dirty, threatening public environment with travel almost impossible and with countless people living in the streets – but with a few incongruous splendid set pieces, like escapist islands in a sea of pollution. In short, an environment of private affluence and public squalor, and with no effective means of controlling it." He called for a new agenda which would "elevate the needs and aspirations of ordinary people above a combination of rampant profiteering... and arrogant professional individualism."

Eleanor Heartney, 'What's missing at Battery Park?', *Sculpture,* 1989

Urban regeneration schemes in New York have prompted similar responses. Battery Park City has been much praised for its "uncompromising" commissioning and siting of public art. But according to critic Eleanor Heartney, the art itself is implicated in the development's reputation as a "playground for the privileged."

Richard Artschwager, *Sitting/Stance*. **Photo:** Art on File International

Sited in 1989 at Thames Street and The Esplanade in New York's Battery Park, it comprises over-sized furniture in an implied triangular room. The furniture consists of two lounge chairs, two 9' granite chairs and two stainless-steel picnic tables.

Art constituency & community

The Strategy for Public Art in Cardiff Bay lists the benefits of employing visual arts consultants and artists in regeneration schemes, the former holding the "key" to "achieving and maintaining a high-quality programme", the latter usually "spearheading the process of urban regeneration... central to the successful marketing of a city's cultural image." Artists' professional involvement is a significant factor in determining the commercial, environmental and cultural success of building programmes and regenerative schemes. Their early involvement in projects results in a "greater harmony between artworks and their settings". Residencies in community settings are an "extraordinarily successful means of creating firm relationships between artists and public". Developments in public art offer artists creative opportunities – "the more successful programmes have not shied away from the radical and innovatory" – qualities often regarded by the artistic community as synonymous with excellence in the visual arts.

A survey of artists' attitudes for this book revealed that while the majority regarded working in settings outside the gallery as a personal challenge, they were committed to forging a relationship with the public – reaching "vast numbers of people who never visit galleries", engaging "with society", working collaboratively, "improving and humanising settings". Yet over the years, Arts Council policies have often had the effect of polarising the interests of artists and the public.

The council's tradition of supporting professional practice was clear from the early catalogues for open-air sculpture exhibitions – from 1948 onwards – which called for audiences to make concessions to works which required "a wide tolerance and understanding." For years, it was considered unnecessary to provide interpretative support for those who floundered when confronted by modern art. The cult of the artist which this engendered still persists amongst some sectors of the art world. For example, the 1990 *TSWA Four Cities Project: New Works for Different Places* was intended to "establish a space in which artists might respond and make new work." The catalogue introduction only makes a passing reference to communities into which artists and works were parachuted. Organiser James Lingwood, explained: "The directional

Richard Serra, *Tilted Arc.* **Photo:** Art on File International

Sculpture in Cor-Ten steel, by the Jacob K Kravitz building, Foley Square, New York.

pull of most community arts has been towards a lowest common denominator... I'm not interested in commissioning projects which have at their base the need not to displease.... On the contrary... they have to be prepared to displease."

A similarly paternalistic viewpoint characterised Helen Chadwick's attitude to the 1992 BBC Art Billboard project. "I'm working quite selfishly. It's not campaigning on my part. I'd like to look at things that give me a frisson, speak about my experience. Maybe I'm the sole consumer. If it resonates with anyone else out there, great."

The principle of art needing no justification outside itself has provoked resentment on the part of the public, particularly in respect of public art and more so with permanent rather than temporary manifestations. A notorious example is Richard Serra's *Tilted Arc* which crossed the entire square between the Federal Building and the Courthouse, Manhattan. The artist intended it to block the view to and from the street, and "encompass the people who walk on the plaza in its volume.... After the piece is created, the space will be understood

Willow Walk by Richard Harris for 'New Forms in Willow'. **Photo:** the artist

Projects Environment which investigates ways artists and others use creativity to address world urban and rural environmental crises, organised 'New Forms in Willow' in 1990, a programme of residencies, workshops and conference centred around Wirral's Ness Gardens where willows are still grown for basket-making.

primarily as a function of the sculpture." Installed in 1981, the work was greeted with marked hostility. A petition demanding its removal was signed by 1,300 employees in the complex. People objected to being involuntarily involved: some regarded the work as a symbol of incipient totalitarianism. After a court hearing in 1985, the commissioning agency agreed to resite it. In 1989 it was destroyed.

The polarisation of the artistic and non-artistic communities has led to incidents of abuse to public art – even lack of appreciation of it – which are conventionally described as 'ignorant' or 'mindless'. Whatever the criminal implications, such responses may be triggered by symbolic values attributed to works which do not necessarily pertain to their formal or aesthetic qualities, but to extra-aesthetic characteristics. In the case of public art, these may reflect the initial impact of the work on the community, the nature of their introduction to it, their lack of comprehension of it or detachment from it, their objections to the values it represents or the circumstances of its siting. By the same token, the symbolic values that accrue to public art works explain why some come to be adopted as logos by local institutions whilst others are vandalised.

Log seat commissioned by Sustrans from Jim Partridge and Liz Walmsley, sited on the cycle path between Bristol and Bath.
Photo: John Grimshaw

In selecting sculpture, Sustrans often commissions artists whose work is environmentally friendly and who recycle materials. Over £200,000 has already been spent on commissions. It won the 1992 British Gas/Arts Council 'Working for Cities' Art in Public Places award for work in Strathclyde, Avon and N E England.

There are evidently considerable problems inherent in addressing non-specific regional, national and international audiences. What kind of subject matter might reflect common interests and aspirations, if indeed these exist? One function ascribed to public art is that it should amuse the public. Isabel Vasseur, curator of the sculpture programmes at Gateshead and Glasgow garden festivals described the excitement of "putting something up that's going to be seen by such a cross-section of the public. The people who come are relaxed and happy. They're having a day out."

The ambitions of other public art works are more serious, if not longer-term. In the same way that some planners stress the importance of taking into account the value people attach to landscapes, nature and places, certain public artworks are conscienciously conceived to engender

Sculpture in coppiced willow and hazel by Chris Drury made for East Sussex's Cuckoo Summit coinciding with the 1992 Earth Summit. Photo: Paul Grivell

For an event which linked global themes and environmental issues with the development of Sustrans' Heathfield/ Polegate cycle path, artists chose an issue relevant to the summit linked with the locality, incorporated the concept of sustainability and worked on site for at least a day with school or community groups to make a permanent or temporary work. This piece is expected to last around three years.

Joanna Morland, *New Milestones*, Common Ground, 1988

local meanings. These are often carried out by professionals working in close consultation with specific communities in ways that flout the standard conventions of appreciation and participation, artist and spectator. The works may be created by that community or involve them closely in some other way. Like Projects Environment's 'New Forms in Willow', they may share some of the educational aspirations of American 'environmentalism'. In marked contrast with 'parachute art', they are relatively less self-referential, more concerned with context.

Public artworks are also commissioned by organisations who might be loth to describe themselves as art promoters, as a device to achieve their missions. Sustrans is one example. It campaigns for changes in transport policy, and over the last twelve years has built some 220 miles of cycle paths which enable the public to travel safely, and without traffic. It commissions sculptures which serve as mile points along its routes.

Another successful example is the organisation Common Ground which, since its inception in 1983, has devised a range of schemes in which artists have imaginatively highlighted conservational and ecological concerns. One such scheme is the series of 'New Milestones' projects. These encourage and assist parish council groups and individuals to commission works "which celebrate and draw attention to part of their place – its history, geology, topography, natural history, people and stories. The works must have meaning for the present-day inhabitants and for future generations and become part of the life of the community."

This is, perhaps, the aspiration which public art commissions in the future should seek to achieve.

Alain Ayers, *The Masham Leaves*, a New Milestones commission in Yorkshire. Photo: the artist

"New Milestones is about what places mean to the people who live in them and about how to express that meaning in an imaginative and accessible way through sculpture. In encouraging landholders or local communities to commission craftspeople and sculptors to crystallize feelings about their place in a public and permanent way, we are not only trying to liberate sculpture into the wild and give anyone courage to commission art and communicate their caring, we are also emphasising that our feelings about everyday landscapes are important and should be taken seriously, that our moment in history has something to offer and that in setting our imagination free to explore places, we can help initiate new cultural touchstones worthy of our time." (Sue Clifford, Common Ground).

2 • Roles & functions

James Peto   'Public' art is never truly public. Works are either privately commissioned or selected by a small number of individuals. The public rarely owns the work and in many cases its audience is limited – as it is in a gallery – to those who frequent its site.

Describing where the art is sited, as opposed to the art itself, as 'public' – as in the title of this book – can prove equally problematic. There are increasingly few genuinely public places. Most work outside the gallery is sited on privately (often corporately) owned property, or on civic property. It seems that art is nonetheless designated 'public' if it is outdoors, preferably accessible or prominent.

The word 'public' has come to refer to its physical or geographical location. I believe this perception, as applied to 'public art', needs to be changed if the potential for artists to contribute in more meaningful ways to the shaping of society and the environment is to be fulfilled.

Specific

For the future, we need to be thinking less about public art in terms of where it is placed, and more about the function it fulfils and how its role could be developed. From the time art first found its way into art galleries up until the late twentieth century movement to encourage work outside the gallery, the majority of works of art for 'public' locations have been designed to fulfil quite specific purposes. A glossary of public artworks in an average British city would for the most part encompass war memorials, monuments to national or local heroes and dignitaries, religious symbols and symbols of, or advertisements for, particular businesses or trades.

The intended function of the majority of more recent public artworks is harder to define. The history of political and funding policies which have shaped the current proliferation of public art has been outlined clearly in the previous chapter; but what of the history of public art-making as it relates to changes in artists' intentions and priorities?

Artists

The recent increase in art outside the gallery gained impetus from a reaction against the perceived '70s elitism of the art gallery as a 'clean white space', and is partly motivated by the desire to reach a larger, broader audience. But for artists there have been other reasons for wanting to work beyond gallery confines. For most, working in the public domain is a means of extending existing practice. Artists who see their work as a vehicle for expressing and communicating ideas or raising questions are constantly searching for and experimenting with new forms of expression – new ways of communicating. Particular sets of circumstances can be found outside the gallery which allow the artist to draw on a wider set of references, whether physical, social or conceptual. Much of Walter de Maria's work from the '60s and '70s could justifiably be described as minimalist and ideally suited to the clean white space, but his best known works of the '70s – as with those of Robert Smithson – were made outside the gallery. Neither artist worked outside the gallery to find a wider public – part of the attraction for Smithson of the site for *Spiral Jetty* was its inaccessibility. The ideas and forms they were exploring were linked with materials which could only be provided by a different environment: the outdoor work was an extension of their regular practice.

Art in public can only remain stimulating if we progress towards an understanding of public which is not dictated by place or location. Is a sculpture sited at Broadgate any more public than one in the collection of the National or Tate galleries? It is a mistake to draw too heavy a distinction between *art*-making and *public* art-making. If public art is viewed as a separate practice, it risks becoming limited to propaganda on the one hand or to purely functional design on the other. Art must be allowed room to be provocative and raise more questions than it can answer.

Installation

As more artists move away from the more formalist approach which suited the neutrality of the clean white space, an interest has developed in 'installations' rather than the display of single objects. These works usually communicate through the interaction of different elements or

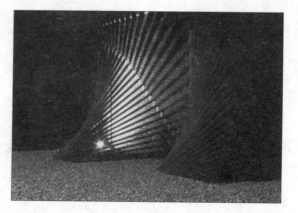

Charles Quick's *Light Wave*, Wakefield Station 1985, a commission initiated by the artist and managed by Public Arts. **Photo:** the artist

materials which then cross-refer in the viewer's mind, according to how s/he associates with them. Outside the comparatively neutral space of the gallery the sets of references and associations which artists can exploit as raw material for their work increase infinitely: not just the associations evoked by the physical environment, but also those inherent in the various systems of social interaction. It is in these very systems that the public realm really lies.

The problem with many late twentieth century examples of public art, especially the permanent ones, is that they appear unconnected to their physical surroundings – for which in many cases they are supposed to compensate – and, more importantly, to the systems and forces shaping those surroundings. Interaction between a formal work and its environs can heighten visual interest. Static sculptures can be made to *work*, whether passively – as in Charles Quick's *Light Wave* commissioned by British Rail for Wakefield Westgate Station, which

Ron Haselden *The Nottingham Sculpture* for the Royal Centre, Nottingham. **Photo:** the artist

Fête by Ron Haselden, **a son et lumière at Plouër-sur-Rance, France in 1992. Photo:** the artist

Originally constructed in a small water-meadow at Feeringbury Manor, Essex where carousels of lights and sound revolved around the meadow suspended from a cluster of willow trees, the piece has also been created for the Serpentine Gallery, The Minories, Canary Wharf and Plouër-sur-Rance.

becomes animated when viewed from a passing train – or actively, as with Ron Haselden's vortex of glowing and fading neon tubes above the entrance to Nottingham's Concert Hall. Haselden intended the apparently random colour changes of the tubes to be sound-triggered, translating the musical and other sound patterns only heard inside the hall into visual patterns only visible outside.

Engagement

The public domain doesn't only increase opportunities for artists to forge relationships between their work and its immediate physical surroundings, but also enables them to engage directly with the social environment: with other people's personal interests, with collective values, political changes, belief systems, changes in the built environment. This might better be described as an engagement with public life.

In the USA, where art in public is a longer established and mainstream activity, there are good models for the production of successful permanent works, exemplified by commissions which are properly integrated into architectural or landscaping schemes. These provide artists with opportunities to contribute to plans for the social function as well as the formal look of the built environment. The history of public art in Britain – in its late twentieth century manifestation – is shorter, but what we do have is a diversity of character and emphasis among organisations involved in programming art in public which should be highly valued and maintained. So too should the burgeoning tradition of artist-led initiatives in the public domain. Public art making and commissioning must not become restrained and institutionalised. In the American magazine *Artforum* in 1988, Patricia C Phillips warned of the

Patricia C Phillips,
Artforum, December,
1988

emergence of a 'public art machine'. "To weave one's way through its labyrinthine network of proposal submissions to appropriate agencies, filings and refilings of budget estimates, presentations to juries, and negotiations with government or corporate sponsors, requires a variety of skills that are frequently antithetical to the production of a potent work of art." It is essential to encourage models of practice which allow artists to exploit a greater range of sites and working methods, rather than circumscribing their practice.

It is nevertheless possible to work within commissioning machinery without becoming subsumed by it. Although embarking on a commission inevitably involves working through systems which can present a multitude of drawbacks – particularly if a variety of interested parties needs to be pleased – working from within and engaging with such systems can create stimulating opportunities.

For example, the functions of local government and administration themselves are fascinating and vital facets of public life and interaction. Opportunities arise as more local authorities in Britain adopt percent for art policies – although unfortunately in many cases, these are only 'in principle' policies until companies contracted by a council can be persuaded to incorporate the one per cent into a particular building commission. But encouraging artists to engage with local government functions would provide opportunities for a truly 'public' art. As well as being in a position to provide practical assistance – engineering and landscaping expertise, site permissions, outdoor electricity, etc – authorities operate many of the economic, social and practical systems which shape our daily lives.

A programme of residencies across government departments – from economic development units through planning and architecture and the engineers' departments – would present opportunities for artists to stimulate awareness, understanding and discussion of these systems. For example, for several years Mierle Ukeles has been an unsalaried artist-in-residence with New York City's Department of Sanitation, developing projects involving the community of sanitation workers as well as the refuse itself and the processes of collecting and disposal. Her work culminated in the construction of *Flow City*, a series of sequential, participatory environments and observation points. These encourage the public to watch the daily workings of a Marine Transfer Facility and consider the wider implications of this vast plant which efficiently transfers Manhattan's garbage into barges and relocates it to other parts of the city. Ukeles' interventions, supported by the department and aided by the plant's architects, consist of glass viewing platforms, corridors constructed partly out of recyclable garbage and a bank of video

Flow City, drawing for public art/video environment at 59th St Marine Transfer station by Mierle Ukeles. Photo: Courtesy Ronald Feldman Fine Arts, New York

monitors providing live views of different parts of the plant and information regarding waste disposal and related environmental issues.

Ukeles' creative interventions uncover the possible wider significance of an apparently banal, everyday process and help to raise public awareness of the interconnectivity of all urban systems.

Artists' projects for the public realm need not necessarily be realised in order to prove engaging and effective. Hypothetical schemes – such as the commissioning of a number of artist/architect collaborations to propose model redesigns for a particular inner city area – have proved successful in stimulating public debate amongst citizens about how they see their immediate environment. Artists involved in the Form and Function project in Philadelphia were asked to "consider themselves as researchers rather than in competition for a commission, and to respond to the civic context.... Ideas came first here, and as money is found many of them are being implemented."

Joanna Griffin 'The Philadelphian Story', *Artists Newsletter*, March 1991

Language

Whether working within the machinery of public life or whether operating outside it, artists working in public have to deal with how the private language of their work – their iconography, if you like – relates to their or someone else's perception of the nature of 'public' language. In the previous chapter, Sara Selwood implies criticism of the "paternalistic"

Helen Chadwick's **billboard** *Wreath to Pleasure* for the BBC Billboard Art Project sited outside the BBC TV Centre. A detail of the image is shown on the cover of the book. Photo: the artist

attitude which she feels is exemplified by Helen Chadwick's admission of "working quite selfishly" and single-mindedly "speaking about [her] own experience" when making work for the 1992 BBC Billboard Art Project. This criticism implies incompatibility of the artist's 'private' visual language with that of the 'public', and denies the all-important interrelationship between the two.

By its very nature, the public is indefinable: a collection of different individuals in different places at different times, their relationships constantly shifting. It is impossible to second-guess the public especially when making billboard works produced in multiples for different sites. One approach to making billboard images is to use the language and image-making techniques of an advertising campaign to put across a message or raise particular questions. Another is to create, as Helen Chadwick did, an image of personal significance with a strong resonance for the artist who designed it. If an image is well conceived and strong it will resonate with other individuals. Public language, like public life, is not fixed and constantly crosses over with the 'private'.

Mary Miss, when asked if it was possible when working in the public domain to make something that reflected communal values, said for her it would have been a presumptuous goal: "I'm really thinking of the individual very much when I'm making these and I'm trying to make very private experience possible in a public space." Any work whose visual language is predetermined by an assumption on the part of the artist or commissioning agent of the nature of public taste is as liable to public

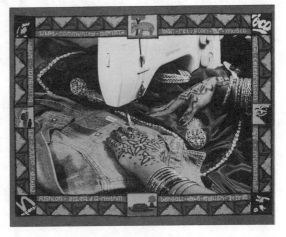

West meets East, a 16' x 20' photo-mural created as a collaboration between Loraine Leeson and students from Central Foundation School. **Photo:** Art of Change

Many urban communities are visually dominated by advertising hoardings imposing their images and values. Community InSight, an aspect of the work of the Art of Change (formerly Docklands Community Project), enables artists to work in a community framework and provides radical visual interventions to social and environmental issues. For this billboard at Wapping, an 8" x 10" negative of the image was blown up and sealed in perspex. This protects it against weather and the UV filter prevents colour fading. The process is guaranteed for three years. "Advantages are that all post-production goes on in the lab, and full colour can be used; maintenance costs are reduced and images can be circulated between hoarding sites with less risk of damage."

rejection as one which derives from an artist's individual interests and iconography.

Stefan Gec's *Trace Elements,* commissioned for the 1990 TSWA 'Four Cities' project, is an example of a work rooted in personal (or 'private') history but which also linked with events of public and international significance. In 1942 Gec's Ukrainian father had been forced by the advancing German army to leave home and family to work as a labourer in Austria. The war over, the political situation in the Soviet Union made it impossible for him to return home. In 1990, learning that eight Soviet submarines decommissioned after the thawing of the Cold War had been brought to Northumberland to be scrapped, Gec had eight bells cast from steel from the submarines' hulls. These symbols of warning or mourning as well as of celebration were hung at water level beneath Newcastle's High Level Bridge, disappearing slowly as

Jenny Holzer's
work *PT119* for
Leicester Square
Underground
Station, 1988/89,
courtesy of the
Artangel Trust.
Photo: David
Godbold, Marcus
Hansen & Laurie
Sparham

the water rose, tolling unseen and unheard beneath the incoming tide, resurfacing again a little more rusted with every ebbing tide. A plaque attached to railings on the quayside showed a map of Northern Europe including the Soviet Union and Newcastle with pictograms of submarines etched beside the names of Soviet ports and the text: "The metal from eight Soviet submarines."

Without access to catalogue explanation of Gec's personal connection to the Cold War and the collapse of the Soviet Union, it could be argued that the viewer is denied access to some of the work's potentially rich associations. I would argue that the strength of the work is that the image of the eight bells resurfacing from the deep like

Stefan Gec *Trace Elements*,
1990. Photo: Stephen White

Bench and light standards at Pearlstone Park, Baltimore, 1985 by Scott Burton. **Photo:** Art on File International

The artist designed these along an esplanade on a site which was formerly a traffic island, and also designed the entire park.

problems that won't go away, is resonant enough to encourage the public to form their own 'private' associations.

Integration

For Scott Burton, designer of a variety of successfully integrated outdoor projects, there was no room in public art for private language. He believed "forms of art that are not fine art are the only ones that have a chance of being disseminated into the wider culture." Therefore, "what office workers do in their lunch hour is more important than my pushing the limits of my self-expression." He preferred to envisage "a new kind of relationship (between audience and artwork)... beginning to evolve... toward a visual culture of design and applied art." Burton saw public commissions as an opportunity to help create a socially useful environment. His work operates almost covertly, a discreetly harmonious but functional street furniture that encourages social interaction and caters for a set of specific needs.

Scott Burton's work is built to last, to please and to 'fit in'. Many artists as committed as he to a socially engaged public art prefer to adopt a more provocative role, questioning accepted versions of history, illuminating hidden functions of public institutions and disturbing preconceptions about systems that govern public life. Their practice demands the urgency and topicality of the temporary.

Temporary

Where much of the work of Burton, Mary Miss and Jackie Ferrara is concerned with the invention of a new and permanent architecture for the street, Polish-born artist Krzysztof Wodiczko's *Homeless Projections* of the late '80s question the perceived meanings of architecture and give new significance to the monuments of city streets and those who live in their shadows.

Existing in their primary form for just three or four nights in a beam of light, Wodiczko's projections allow him to achieve an urgency and topicality on the street. The nature of imagery and technique is such that the work crystallizes in photographic reproduction: the temporary is thus guaranteed a degree of permanence and broad circulation through display in galleries – in the form of framed or re-projected photographs – or through books, magazines and postcards. Wodiczko projected images of the homeless, or of attributes of homelessness, onto monuments in Boston, transforming the homeless themselves into new city monuments. More recently, with prototypes for *Homeless Vehicle* he has found a way for his art to develop a more permanent function, at once symbolic and useful.

In a time of accelerating change in public life, the making of permanent work that can remain urgent and achieve a lasting relevance presents an enormous but invigorating challenge. The temporary allows an artist to address a specific social or physical context at a specific time. It reduces the fear of failure and encourages experimentation. Those angered by the work can be partially placated by the knowledge that it won't be with them for long, and vandalism is at least a short-term rather than long-term problem.

Krzysztof Wodiczko *Homeless Vehicle*, 1989. **Photo:** Exit Art

Monument against Fascism in
Hamburg-Harburg, 1986 by
Esther and Jochen Gerz.
Photo: Kulturbehörde Hamburg

In 1986 Jochen and Esther Gerz collaborated with city officials
in Hamburg-Harburg, Germany, on a project which succeeded in
establishing immediate relevance, relied on participation of local citizens
for its completion, incorporated a certain amount of 'vandalism' into its
form and character, and which, though it will mutate over the first years
of its life, will remain as a permanent work. Their *Monument against
Fascism* a thirty foot tall, lead-coated, square column, was erected in
front of city council buildings. Passers-by were invited to sign their
names into the column's soft surface in agreement with a displayed text
emphasising personal political responsibility. The column soon became
a graffiti board attracting, beside the supporting signatures, pro-fascist
and other slogans, bearing witness to the currency and strength of
conviction of both sides of a moral argument.

This memorial refuses to stand as a confident, authoritative
symbol, confining issues and events to past memories and setting them
safely in stone. As the writing space around the column fills up, so the

Part of *The Wilds and the Deep* project by Martha Fleming and Lyne Lapointe, **New York 1990. Photo:** the artists

For this project in a disused ferry terminal produced under the aegis of Creative Time Inc, the work comprised a slave ship model painted life-size on canvas, laid out on the roof of the building, visible from the skyscrapers of the financial district and from air traffic into Manhattan heliport next door.

column is lowered into its foundation. The 'buried' section can still be viewed underground through a window. Eventually the column will be reduced to a flat lead square, flush with the paving.

If permanent work runs the risk of becoming outmoded or irrelevant in the future, much of the most interesting temporary work has set out to make the past live in the present, and to show the contemporary relevance of the past. The working processes of Canadian artists Martha Fleming and Lyne Lapointe began in their local neighbourhood in Montreal. Their first collaborative work involved negotiating access to an abandoned fire station and working with the building over an extended period, researching its history and installing works related to their interpretation of its significance, both past and present.

Similar projects have since taken place in other buildings which have a significant public function – post office, theatre, ferry terminal, immigration point – described by the artists as "ideologically, socially, emotionally and economically charged architectures, chosen with care as integral parts of the work."

For example, *La Donna Delinquenta*, completed over a three year period, inhabited a vaudeville theatre abandoned 20 years earlier. Fleming and Lapointe integrated their work within the building's architecture and ornamentation, drawing directly onto the walls, using sound and light effects and creating a series of installed tableaux related either directly or indirectly to the role of the building as a place of spectacle now abandoned. Working closely with current neighbours and former users of the chosen buildings, their work deliberately addresses issues relevant to these people and ultimately involves re-opening the building to the public, raising awareness of its potential. In refreshing

Andy Goldsworthy's *Maze*, made for the site of the former Eden Pit along the Consett and Sunderland Sustrans cycle path. Photo: Northern Arts

contrast to those who presume some mythical benchmark of what is publicly acceptable and accessible, Fleming and Lapointe believe that "the more you trust an audience and the more you give them, the more mutual respect there is."

Their work also incorporates imagery from art and natural history and from the histories of philosophy, psychology and science, the artists viewing these as an integral part of the context they are addressing, one to which they insist the immediate public can relate, through familiarity with the imagery used if not with the art works themselves.

Mediation

There is a danger however, when art 'moves in' to the public realm and is felt to be speaking an exclusive language, that its reception will reinforce a perception of art world elitism. Counteracting it depends on the way in which mediation between the work and the public is conducted and it is vital an artist is clear about his/her intentions, and that they are understood by those commissioning or facilitating the work. Whether a work is first and foremost an experiment, or an expression of a very personal experience, or a deliberate attempt to communicate with as broad an audience as possible, an artist must be sure of his/her reasons for applying for a particular commission or choosing a particular environment in which to work, and clear about how the work is intended to function. As well as strengthening the work, such clarity helps in the vital role of mediation.

Mediation, however, is a continuous process which involves care not only in introducing a work to its public but also in the way it is documented and how discussion surrounding it is conducted. These factors greatly influence a work's reception. To mediate between an artwork and its audience does not necessarily mean spending hours asking members of the immediate community what sort of art they would like to see – although many successful public works have been shaped through a process of consultation and collaboration. Nor does it entail every public artwork being accompanied by a detailed explanation of 'what it means'.

However, because no territory is neutral and placing an artwork in a public site may be seen as laying claim to that space, artists need to be prepared to listen to those expected to live in close contact with their work. Although the level of consultation necessary depends on the context, the work's producers must attempt to anticipate and appreciate its possible social impact and the criteria by which it might be judged. The best means of gaining this understanding is likely to be discussion on the ground with those whose lives are part of the circumstances for which the work is to be made. Such conversations also encourage the public's interest in the work and understanding of the artist's relationship to the work's context. Should controversy arise – a likelihood with any work that engages with the contradictions of public life – artists who have fully investigated the work's context are best prepared to mediate productively.

The *Tilted Arc* affair described in the previous chapter was disastrous not only because of lack of consultation with users of Federal Plaza before the siting of the piece – the work was commissioned by a government agency, the General Services Administration, based in another city, Washington – but also as result of the way in which the controversy was mediated. Public hearings set up by advocates for removal of the sculpture skilfully exploited popular discontent by staging arguments for and against as if they were between those who thought they knew best (the 'art experts') and those who were supposed not to understand (the plaza's users), thus stirring greater resentment towards the work amongst the latter. By taking the moral high ground, many of its defenders allowed themselves to fall into this trap.

Tilted Arc was a provocative response to what Serra described as a "pedestal site" – a rather brutal and functionless plaza, a difficult location for any artwork. In order to encourage a truly engaged public art, we must move away from the idea that the 'public' in art in public refers to such sites, and discard the limited notion of public space as one which is solely physical or geographical. Nor should we think of the public simply as the art's intended consumers, but rather as "the body of ideas

Patricia C Phillips, *Art Journal*, Winter 1989 and subjects that artists chose to concentrate on" – a shifting network of complex relationships between private individuals, corporate bodies and civic systems.

If public art can – through processes of investigation, articulation and re-appraisal – intervene creatively in this network of relationships and can encourage private individuals to question where and how they fit into it, then it has the potential to help shape public life. Since it cannot represent the truth to everyone, art in public should seek to encourage the sound of contradictory voices.

3 • Attributes & attitudes

Brian Baker   Although artists, clients, agents and design and construction professionals may place the emphasis on different elements, there is broad consensus on key attitudes and attributes needed by artists when undertaking commissions for public sites.

Crucial qualities

Assertiveness and persistence are crucial qualities, needed both in the processes of obtaining work and in its successful delivery. Equally important are good communication skills which are at the hub of any multi-disciplinary project. Artist Sue Ridge, who has undertaken many complex commissions in the last twelve years, says: "There is nothing worse than pretending it will be all right on the night." Her policy is to work in close and continuing contact with engineers and architects, so that problems are foreseen and addressed directly.

"It's the need for artists to articulate clearly what their ideas and wishes for the project are," says Tessa Jackson, former organiser of the visual arts programme during Glasgow's 1990 City of Culture year. Now looking at the public art commissioning world from the outside as director of Bristol's Arnolfini Gallery, she emphasises: "Things should not be left unsaid."

Public Art Commissions Agency (PACA) director Vivien Lovell feels that "by choosing to work in this way, an artist puts themself in the public realm" and she reflects: "Some are better at taking criticism than others." She believes artists need to accept that "the nature of public art is itself contentious."

If this seems to build barriers for the introverted and inexperienced, take heart, it doesn't have to. Lovell declines to be prescriptive. "We work with a spectrum of artists, from people who get on with everyone to those who are quiet but produce stunning work. Context and consultation are important but there are different forms for achieving that." She thinks

Section of Anu Patel's **railings on Bath Row for the St Thomas Peace Gardens, Birmingham.**
Photo: the artist

Previously known for her sculpture and works on paper, an inspiration for this work was the Bengali tradition of paper-cutting in which animal or floral motifs are chiselled through 20 or 30 sheets of paper simultaneously giving the final product a serial, frieze-like effect when shaken out.

commissioning agencies have a valuable role, speaking for and negotiating on behalf of artists who are not that assertive. It's not always the experienced who are best at the selection process either.

Anu Patel has obtained a sequence of commissions in Birmingham in recent years. Her most complex with the largest budget, the new Peace Gardens scheme, was her first. Despite now being experienced at handling interviews, she still finds them traumatic. "Each situation is different. The interview is as much about responding to the interviewers as about presentation of the ideas."

For a commission at Nechells Library, a deprived multi-cultural area, PACA arranged for four short-listed artists to give a presentation. In preparation, Patel visited the neighbourhood to talk informally with library users and other local residents. For the presentation – which won her the commission – she illustrated her ideas with drawings, described how the designs would be accessible to the local community and gave initial thoughts about how the work might be made.

Changing attitudes

Architects for the interior refurbishment of the library felt an artist shouldn't be involved. "They doubted the abilities of artists to cope with these situations and became more negative when we suggested that the designs should be exhibited in the library to seek people's opinions." Patel, like others involved in commissions for public spaces, has found some architects fearful of turning down public opinion, preferring not to

Sandi Kiehlmann's
January banner.
Photo:
Needleworks

ask. She feels, however, artists should be in the forefront, suggesting solutions to deal with these sensitive areas.

Working with the public, in public, or attempting to put over the idea of a piece of work to people living near or regularly passing the location, can prove a testing challenge for an artist. Sandi Kiehlmann, a textile artist whose commissions are being realised in public, and with participation by the public, enjoys the collaboration. She was one of the designers and facilitators working on twelve large banners for the 'Keeping Glasgow in Stitches' project in 1990. This involved practical contributions from nearly 2000 people, though most of the sewing was done by fairly regular volunteers and the process co-ordinated through Needleworks' community programme.

Her initial contribution was to design the 'January' banner, depicting the sales. Each banner had to reflect a particular month and was made during that month. The first artist commissioned, she feels, perhaps inevitably, that she was the guinea pig. It was also her first public commission, so she felt she had to stick to the agreed brief. Sponsors the *Glasgow Herald* gave her access to their photo library for source material. Although she would have liked to change some elements, she felt she ought to stick to the plan. But during the sewing stage everything was freer. "I got the women to add in their own design ideas. I didn't worry about them changing it too much."

She believes artists, when working with a group of enthusiasts, need to be open, optimistic, never daunted, to listen and to make sure participants both enjoy and learn from the experience. To acclimatise people who will make a significant contribution to the production of banners, she takes the sewing machines apart to show how they work.

Production

Paula Woof, who used to believe in producing her murals on site, now feels it "can take up too much time and lower your concentration too much. It can be physically hard." Now she favours working on site one day a week when the schedule and nature of the job can accommodate it, linking the commission with a residency either on site or nearby, and setting up a display of drawings and previous work at the location to generate feedback. For a series of panels at Wolverhampton Station, she painted the first on site with clear benefits to her: it helped her to learn more about the subject matter and also gave momentum to the rolling fundraising programme for the project.

Relationships were difficult initially and both perseverance and personality were important. "People are naturally suspicious and the ice

Southampton Station mosaic mural by Sue Ridge. Photo: the artist

Sue Ridge's Southampton Station mural was multi-sponsored with two local authorities and BR's Community Unit prominent. Commissioning agents Public Art Development Trust suggested the concept of looking both back and forward through references to the city's past and present might be realised using ceramics. The success of the project boosted support for art in public within the city council and helped secure budgets for the Public Art Officer post. Ridge introduced artist-blacksmith Alan Evans to the clients at Southampton. The resulting artists' collaboration – in which Evans' designed and made forged steel gates for the doorway at the centre of the mosaic – enhanced the quality of the work. Ridge has since worked with Evans on projects in Leicester and London.

had to be broken." She uses the staff mess, and railway staff will now ask her how much it would cost to do a portrait for them, although like most people, they consider a fair price expensive.

Traditional male-dominated worlds like the railway – despite the increased number of women working in them – test the artist. Woof says "they like to fantasize and gossip. You have to keep above it."

Organisation

Although assertiveness is a key attribute, Sue Ridge has also realised "you have to learn a lot of other skills." She feels that artists working regularly on public commissions "have to be as organised as architects." In particular, she says, in writing everything down. Tessa Jackson's view is that "all on a team have a responsibility to ask questions early on. Discontent develops when they fail to do so." She asks: "If the artist doesn't like the way the work is lit did s/he say initially they wanted to be involved in those decisions?"

It doesn't follow however that if everything is raised well in advance and detailed in writing that the artist will always get what they want, especially on a tight, multi-layered contract. At Southampton Station, where Ridge undertook a mosaic mural, she queried the lighting quality. The initial response was there was no money to enhance it. Later, project managers suggested they could find money for the lighting by taking the floor replacement out of the scheme. "I said leave the lighting and renew the floor. There is no point in highlighting a concrete floor."

Persistence

But it is worthwhile being persistent in trying to solve a problem, especially in long-term phased schemes. In Newarke underpass in Leicester, where Ridge has designed mosaics with the aid of computers, lighting engineers installed unsatisfactory exposed conduits in the first phase. They may be changed by her persistently pressing the point as the scheme rolls on. "You don't always win battles in the public realm. You just basically try to get the best you can and in long-term jobs, keep on trying. You can't specify everything."

Developing skills

Public Art Commissions Agency believes commissioning agencies play a major role in generating opportunities for artists to stretch their medium. For example, Anu Patel learned about working in metal through the demands of the Peace Gardens commission.

For the Tabor School project, to fulfil consultant artist Michael Brennand Wood's intention to create opportunities for artists to work in new materials or on a dramatically different scale, metalworker and jeweller David Watkins was commissioned to design a sculpture for the front of the building, and Maura Heslop – normally a maker of small-scale metal brooches and earrings – has produced free-standing cut-metal relief sculptures.

Environment

Environmental artist Valerie Pragnell's collaborators are often conservationists. On a practical level, they are foresters. Chain saw operators are a rich seam of information on detailed properties of individual woods. "I need to know about grain and knots and how quickly a wood can be cut." For Pragnell – who also works regularly with blacksmiths – "it's a dialogue, I don't always know the best way to realise my ideas and discussion can help solve technical problems."

Pragnell's two *Oak under Oak* pieces are included in the 1992 Garden Festival Wales. Made at Margam Sculpture Park, they are placed in an area of established oak trees in the woodland part of the site. The pieces are seen in profile as you approach. The branches form an upwards shape under the trees, depicting renewal and regeneration. Although Pragnell would like them to remain in situ, after-use of the site will dictate which commissions stay.

Integration

The way in which visual artists have contributed to garden festivals since they first began reflects the shift towards an integrated approach. Garden Festival Wales Project Manager Adrian Poller says: "At previous festivals there was a vast amount of work on site. We went for involving

Developing skills

Undertaking a commission involves using a complex combination of arts and business skills. Commissions often involve managing large sums of public money, and an artist's reputation will suffer irreparable damage if lack of artistic, financial, technical or management experience results in a poorly received piece of work.

Courses

At undergraduate level, many more degree courses incorporate placements and projects. Two examples are at London's Central St Martin's – where students on the Fine Art and Critical Studies BA course learn all aspects of planning, funding and carrying out a piece of work, using public places such as a café, laundrette or shops as their site – and Winchester School of Art – where Fine Art BA students can select in their second year to spend 20% of their time on a 'public art' option which includes talks by artists, curators and project managers and placements with project in public settings. Glasgow School of Art's BA in Environmental Art provides students with a grounding in project management, and includes the inititiation, development and documentation of a project from proposal to a completed art work.

There are also a number of part or full-time specialist post-graduate courses on which artists gain technical, business and presentational skills as well as the chance to undertake commissions and public projects with the support and guidance of more experienced artists. These include Duncan of Jordanstone's MFA – which now incorporates the Public Art course – and Chelsea's MA in Public Art and Design – which attracts artists, makers, architects, planners and others "who are involved in the conception and implementation of public schemes."

Other methods

For many artists, however, higher education is not appropriate, and artists are using are a variety of other formal and informal methods to gaining experience and respond to the needs of a particular commission.

Apprenticeship

There are still few formal apprenticeships offered to artists who want to develop the skills needed for working to commission whilst working under the guidance of more established artists. The Investment in the Future of Fine Art in Public Places survey of London-based

Seat at Gregynog, University of Wales made by Jim Partridge and Liz Walmsley. **Photo:** Martin Roberts

Made from oak grown on the estate and sited under a sycamore canopy to provide shelter and a resting place, this commission was organised by Artwork Wales/ Cywaith Cymru and part-funded by the Countryside Council for Wales.

organisations involved in art in public by Loraine Leeson in 1990 showed that although 37% offered formal placements, only 4% provided apprenticeships. Reasons for this included the problems of obtaining funding for such training and the gulf between the skills and expectations of graduates and the realities of working to commission. "Work on offer generally demands a wide range of skills – social and organisations as well as visual – which are not normally taught on fine art courses."

However, as part of the St Peter's Riverside Sculpture Project in Sunderland, where artist/consultant Colin Wilbourn's brief is to identify suitable sites for sculpture, seating and railings, an apprenticeship has been created. Funded by Wearside Training and Enterprise Council and others, Karl Fisher – who comes from an industry rather than arts background – is spending a year developing skills in woodcarving, stone carving, metalwork, modelling and also learning how to run a small business, the intention being to help him become a self-employed artist.

New materials

For some commissions, artists need to gain experience with using new materials. For example, Mark Renn's *Garden of Hope* commission in 1989 for a community garden in the village of Sedgley in the West Midlands involved decorative gates and a cast concrete poem. To work effectively in concrete he needed to formally experiment with colouring and casting techniques and arranged to spend a month training with artist Michael Farrell. The resulting piece was cast on site by the two artists and a team of volunteers.

In 1992, when jeweller Jenni Neal was designing railings for a Wimpey Homes Development in Middlesbrough, her initial ideas were worked up collaboratively with artist/blacksmith Peat Oberon,

Detail from the *New Dolphin Mooring Post* **created by Freeform artists** Graham Robinson, Richard Broderick, Sally Brown and Sue Woolhouse **for North Shields' Fish Quay. Photo:** Stan Gamester

who helped her to learn the practical constraints of cost and construction limitations. During fabrication, she also worked in the forge to get hands-on experience of blacksmithing.

Longer-term policies

Artist-led organisation Arts Resource has recognised the value of bringing in artists with specialist skills from outside the region to respond to the needs of specific commission briefs, and linked this with the need for artists in the locality to enhance their skills and broaden their experience to enable them to apply for a broader range of commissions in the future.

When Jim Partridge was commissioned to make four seats along the River Wear, sculptor Jim Roberts worked with him and a team of workers supplied by Sunderland Training Agency. Roberts' role fell into two parts. Firstly he was "mediator" for Partridge – he was born, bred and had studied in the city and knew the site's social and industrial background. Secondly, he could learn a great deal from working for several weeks alongside an artist with considerable experience of siting functional works in public. Partridge too found it a learning experience. The training agency supplied 'brickies' instead of 'chippies' as the work gang, and his ideas for predominantly wood seating were thus developed to include stonework in a more substantial way.

Teamwork

For artist-led Freeform Arts Trust, established over 20 years ago, a major policy is to create commissions in which teams of artists and architects can work together to help people to make their communal spaces – playgrounds, streets, gardens – work better for them. As well as placements for undergraduates, the company provides work experience for graduates in the techniques and practices of indoor and outdoor mural making, the design and construction of playgrounds and gardens and the development of environmental improvement projects involving architects and landscape designers.

"This ensured the aesthetic foundations... were informed by visual artists at a stage where meaningful suggestions could be considered and, in some cases, incorporated into the design. An aesthetic philosophy of co-operation between artists and design professionals... was put in place." *(Alchemy)*

artists in the planning process. It worked well." In 1989, when eight design teams of landscape architects, quantity surveyors and engineers were established, an artist was appointed to each.

For Visual Arts Officer Maggie Gilson, "the essence is collaborative, bringing together a network of creative minds who all had something to bring to the feast we were cooking." For *Obelisk* Denys Short worked closely with Derek Crossland, one of British Steel's top scientists and expert on the properties of stainless steel, and also with fabricator Brian Rands of GBS Engineering. Crossland became enthused with the challenge and regularly travelled 300 miles to contribute.

Tessa Jackson foresees a future for art in public in which people with different expertise initiate schemes which utilise artists and makers at the centre of the process after being inspired by their initial collaborative experience. She cites as an example the new public open space created at Garnethill in Glasgow for the City of Culture celebrations. Conceived as a gift by the German Goethe Institute, landscape artist/architect Dieter Magnus led the project.

After the Goethe Institute offered funds for artist's fees for a permanent memorial to 1990 City of Culture, Magnus was invited to

Denys Short *Obelisk* commissioned for Garden Festival Wales 1992. Photo: Patricia Aithie

"The construction of the piece posed some major challenges, not least because stainless steel is an unforgiving medium and few people in this country know enough about its properties to be able to work with it." *(Alchemy)*

Glasgow to look at sites. Demolition of some housing at Garnethill, a multi-cultural area close to Glasgow city centre, created a site opposite a community centre which was chosen for this project. The concept for Garnethill Park was realised in three phases, partly because finance for construction had to be raised piecemeal, much of it from commercial sponsors. The resulting work used bricks from the old Gorbals and includes areas for play, relaxation and performance.

Jackson feels "it was an extraordinary and involved process which stretched people. The artist was exacting and uncompromising but because he was very good at setting out his detailed requirements

Shell by Kathryn Gustafson. **Photo:** the artist

The intention of this piece for the corporate headquarters of Shell at Rueil-Malmaison was to integrate the building with its environment. The project constituted five spaces, the first a sober and monumental stone entrance. Bordered by a linear pool and undulating ribbons of lawn, it symbolises rocks and earth fluids. Emerging from the pool, which is divided in half by a fine edge of water falling seven centimetres across its length, are four masts with flame-like lights. Water slides under the building's entrance and reappears as a cascade falling into the Water Garden which, with plants and shrubs, provides a multitude of colour. Elsewhere, gardens are formed by parallel bands of grass, shrubs and ground cover, punctuated by trees to echo the rhythm of the building's façade.

in advance, we finished the project with mutual respect all round. Genuine commitment came from site foreman, planner, landscape architects, local community leaders and everyone involved because they could see what the whole project was about and no-one was asked to do a job out of context."

Work with planners

Paris-based landscape artist Kathryn Gustafson's large-scale civic space commission at Evry, a new town outside Paris, was designed as a new central focal point because, as with many new towns, the original plan failed to provide a major civic space. She has created a plaza in which the central design concept was 'freedom of expression', a theme drawn from the name of the plaza 'Les Droits d'Hommes'. To achieve the aim of unifying the surrounding disparate buildings, she had to deal with a carriageway passing through the site. By narrowing it and slowing the traffic it gave pedestrians the priority and created a new space where people could gather. Informal performance spaces and three water features accentuated the idea that different types of cultural intervention could happen there.

Time-scale

The capacity to work quickly can be important in commissioned work. The idea for Gustafson's *Meeting Point,* a land sculpture at Marne la Valle near Paris created on 40 hectares with in-fill from a reservoir site,

Time-scale

Established in 1984, Partnership is a North West-based artist-led organisation which creates teams of artists according to the requirements of each project, with Partnership overseeing negotiation, consultation and production of both temporary and permanent works. For this project, lead artist Jem Waygood was overall Project Manager. "We feel that all contact is best made by practitioners with their specialist knowledge of the field of work. All projects are evaluated as a matter of course afterwards so that we can learn and develop our practice in the future. They are stepping stones in the development of Partnership Arts."

Partnership has undertaken many commissions in their region and elsewhere, including work for Central Manchester and Trafford development corporations, and is consultant to Teesside Development Corporation for Hartlepool redevelopment scheme.

Commissioned by J Sainsbury plc for the Burnley store, *Winds of Change* resulted from the borough planning officer's request to improve the appearance of the store when a new road system exposed the building and increased public visibility, planners feeling this 'gateway' to and from the centre did little to enhance the town's image.

The commission brief was to make a site-specific piece for the whole space. Initial ideas, drawn from extensive local research, were exhibited in the store to create a dialogue with local users.

Research involved two primary schools who visited the store and contributed to choosing the theme. *Winds of Change* refers both to the town's windy nature and to its industrial history as a worldwide exporter of textile machinery. In contrast, Sainsbury's sells goods imported from all over the world.

1989
July: Site meeting between Sainsbury's, Burnley Borough Council and representatives from Townley Art Gallery and Mid-Pennine Arts Association. Outline budget suggested of around £30,000.
September/October: Project methodology developed and likely costs approved in principle by Sainsburys. Local authority asked to consider funding landscape project for opposite wall to complete the refurbishment. Positive feedback to this.

1990
Jan-March: Project artists Jon Biddulph and Paula Woof appointed. Feasibility research phase begins after discussions with Sainsbury's on public consultation processes.

Detail from *Winds of Change* at Burnley. Partnership has now completed an entrance for their Portsmouth store and is negotiating commissions for stores in Plymouth and Ipswich.

April: Design proposal presented to Sainsbury's in the form of a report and model, this to be taken to their architectural design committee for approval.

May: Basic approval given, but the committee requires more extensive work around the building.

June: Scheme represented together with sample wall panel so techniques and visual effect can be approved.

September/October: Detailed architectural and engineering service information collated.

November/December: Work begins on site with shot blasting and chiselling the wall. Design for landscaped area gets approval from local authority.

1991

January: Steel fabrication of figures begins. These are galvanised and primed to be delivered on site.

February/March: Amongst snow storms, figures installed and fitted and sprayed with final colour. Paint/primer seen to be blistering due to trapped moisture. All paint removed with stripper and steel wool, new paint system applied successfully. Casting process begins in foundry.

April: Work on planting bed at the foot of the wall begins using a sub-contracted builder. Almost immediately, there are problems with underground services and builder claims for extra costs. Cast objects fitted to wall and lighting installed. Public relations campaign begins for launch in June.

May: Plaque to commemorate the opening designed and cast.

June: Opening event gets national press coverage, speeches and buffet. A good time had by all!

Following this, the borough council-organised reconstruction of the landscape area was completed, to include seating designed by the artists. The total budget for the mural and landscaping scheme was around £72,000.

Keith Alexander's **carved and stained porch for 66-68 Brinkburn Avenue. Photo:** Anna Pepperall

The artist's desire was "to produce a piece of public artwork which relates to and fully involves the community in which it is sited, as well as reflecting that community's interests and concerns." The house, first transferred to the 'Tyne International' exhibition at the Gateshead Garden Festival, was open to the public during the summer of 1991.

Finding it was easy, with Alexander's carved and stained porch and a mosaic garden – depicting the area both as it was in the 18th century (a rural area with sheep and trees) and as it is now in urban Gateshead – providing a 'landmark' to guide people to it.

began when she had a telephone call from the Mayor's office when the rainy season had stopped the work. Could she do anything with the land? Once a model had been produced and the town council given the go-ahead, she had six weeks to accomplish extensive cut and fill movements. Engineers on the contract were helpful, though her most important collaborator was the bulldozer driver. As she was working in extremely slippery clay, the designs had to be re-calculated after work started to the highest slope grades capable of being held by this material.

The result, entirely created with material that would otherwise have been transported off-site, is a tranquil space depicting the meeting of aggressive and soft land movements, yet one engineered to allow for park development in future. From start to finish it took 18 weeks. The commission cost £600,000, the amount the council would otherwise have spent transporting the waste material from the site.

Anu Patel's central panels for the 'Gateways' signage in the Heartlands urban regeneration area of Birmingham exemplified the urgent time-scales sometimes applied to smaller scale work. Councillors, appalled to find that the original gateways designs lacked originality, were seeking an artistic solution to rescue the situation, though they did this late in the day and on a restricted budget. Patel was approached to make proposals for how the appearance could be improved in a simple way. She visited the sites, worked up an idea that could go on a panel in the centre and designed it. Literally, she had to work in days.

"The question raised with urgent commissions is 'will I regret it later?'" For her, though, it fits her desire to take on many different challenges. "I've grown working in public art. There's a very positive side to working with people in other disciplines." Although the Peace Gardens commission was organised through PACA whose support she praises, detailed problem-solving – as in most large schemes – was through direct collaboration with manufacturer, architect, and in particular landscape architect Lynn Sterling.

Collaboration

Keith Alexander's ability to work collaboratively during an eighteen-month residency working with people with learning difficulties and in schools, and its culmination with the House Project, earned him unstinting praise from Gateshead MBC Visual Arts Officer Anna Pepperall. A terraced house was bought for this artist-initiated project by Northern Rock Housing Trust. During the residency, over 500 people and 17 artists were involved in making 40 objects for the house. For example, the 'meal-time' ceiling rose was made by children from a special school who, as part of the making, visited a local manufacturer of ceiling roses. Other groups worked with textiles, glass, wrought iron and ceramics.

Flexibility

Valerie Pragnell's commission for Sustrans Sculpture Trail in Strathclyde in 1991 involved periodic work on site over six months and a school residency which spanned a year. She regularly spoke to passers by about *Langslie Spiral*, a water diversion and drystone amphitheatre on which she worked with specialist drystone wallers. Delays were caused when the charity temporarily ran out of money and because the job's contractors had to fit it in between other work and would turn up when they could.

Although delays and extended schedules can be frustrating and call for patience and resilience from artists, they can be valuable if an artist is working on several projects at once. Paula Woof works to a rough plan for each month, based on a number of days for each project. Working on different jobs at the same time gives her some flexibility between them, making it possible to focus on demanding, creative tasks when she feels best able.

When several jobs are on stream at once Sue Ridge also produces a timetable and divides her time up in tightly defined detail. If

Valerie Pragnell's *Langslie Spiral* at Milepoint 20 near Lochwinnoch along the Paisley-Irvine Sustrans cycle path. **Photo:** the artist

As broken field drains were emptying into the cutting and erosion had swept the bank away, the commission brief was to "make the water interesting". Water is diverted to come through the back of the wall, cascade over a large rock and enter the stream by a rocky spiral.

work on one job is particularly urgent she might do a solid week on that. She warns: "When you are on site, delays cause tremendous problems." She wants to see more concerted pressure from artists so that they, like others, can charge extra for delays which are not of their making.

Crises often arise when the client changes the timetable. For local authority clients this can be because of changes in the rolled forward budget for the financial year. Ridge had to dramatically accelerate her detailed design drawings, one for each panel, for her abstract for the Holloway Circus underpass refurbishment in Birmingham in 1990. This could have been financially disastrous as for a period she had to employ three assistants. However, she reflects she felt comfortable about it because the fee had been set satisfactorily.

Assistant Director of Recreation at Edinburgh District Council, Leslie Evans, suggests that "when an artist is going to work with local government they have to be aware of the problems created by the beaurocracies and budgeting constraints within which local authorities work. Artists need to stand their ground and not be pressurised into changing what they are producing.... Whilst some authorities understand the artist's point of view from working with them," says Evans, "others do not."

Mother Earth by Mick Petts, **one of the lead artists working with design teams to develop Garden Festival Wales sites.** Photo: Charles Aithie

This commission, which grew from a pressing need to deal with a huge pile of slag on the site, is probably the largest landform in Britain created by a contemporary artist.

Teams

It is in large scale projects like the Birmingham Convention Centre, the adjacent Centenary Square and Cathedral Precinct in Wakefield that the attitudes of other design and construction professionals can be most important. Birmingham's Head of City Centre Planning, Geoff Wright, explains: "From a planner's point of view, you are trying to assemble a lot of different inputs on an area, so the role of the artist can complicate matters." For a major local authority client, the attraction of artist involvement can be that "it's value adding in the sense that no in-house discipline would have been able to do the same thing."

Wright warns of the danger in design teams of too many people trying to lead. After a period of quite difficult working relationships over Centenary Square, artist Tess Jaray and former City architect Bill Reed established a fruitful partnership with visions meshing whilst the landscape architects stepped back a pace.

When Wakefield MBC approached Public Arts in 1989 to assemble a short-list of artists for the Cathedral Precinct project they initially wanted design consultancy ideas for the renovation of the floor surface which had to be replaced for technical reasons. At the time, the Transportation and Engineering Department had completed a run of three small town pedestrianisation schemes in-house. Their perception was that they were stale and were concerned that the use of off-the-shelf materials was making every town centre in Britain look the same. Lead engineer Andy Kerr says: "It was civic pride – we wanted something different for Wakefield." Unsurprisingly they chose Jaray, for whom the project must have seemed custom-made.

After working with her for a year, the detailed designs were agreed and finance identified to go ahead with the scheme in three

Terry Wright **was commissioned through British Health Care Arts to make forty 4ft square photographs for St George's Hospital in London which would improve the hospital environment and help users find their destinations.** Images reflect aspects of the English countryside and colours tie in with the building's colour-coding system. They offer a direction-finding system easily learned, particularly by non-English speakers: 'follow the trees to X-ray' for example.

phases. The first, and largest, phase was completed in July 1992. Predominantly a collaboration between Jaray and the engineers' department, in the first phase opportunities were taken to organise the contracts in a way which enabled the artist to work in her preferred way to realise her vision for Cathedral Precinct.

Many of the detailed elements she designed were therefore excluded from the main contract. In a recession, when competitive prices could be obtained, there was benefit to the client in doing this. For Jaray, and for the quality of the final scheme, there was the benefit of more thinking time and the ability to make decisions about the detail of features over a period of time.

Kerr and colleagues have found working in a design team with Jaray over an extended period of concept, detail and contract work very positive. "We've adopted the attitude that she has this skill and we want to use it." They are comfortable with her because "she recognises our skills and we accept her vision." Importantly, "Tess can talk to us in our language." Kerr feels engineer/artist collaborations are particularly productive and harmonious because of the distance between the skills. In his view, architects can suffer ego problems in accepting an artist into a design team.

Sue Ridge also finds it productive to be an integral member of a design team. "I think it's good to be in there – it gives the artist more respect. Otherwise, people think you just choose colours." Leicestershire County Council's Patrick Davis, project manager on her mural project for Newarke underpass, recognises that the success of her mosaics over three phases has evolved into an art-led regeneration programme for the whole area. In 1992 Davis, using the public and political support

Working with industry

In 1988, whilst still a student at the Royal College of Art, Gwen Heeney set out to design a sculpted brick mythical beast for the festival planned for 1992. "I knew most of the projects would be sponsored, so I approached Ibstock Brick Company with preliminary sketches. They agreed to sponsor me for nine months and give me full run of their Bristol factory, using the kiln room as a vast studio and the

A detail from Gwen Heeney's **30 metre long brick-built serpent at Garden Festival Wales.** Photo: the artist

production line to produce any shape or quantity I needed." She then approached GFW with her ideas, and after seeing drawings, model and costings, they agreed to commission the piece. As a result of seeing the work in progress in the factory – where the beast was created in 30,000 carved wet bricks, which were disassembled and numbered before firing – Brunswick Construction sponsored its building, the artist supervising the brick-laying team on site for three months. "This commission was a total collaboration between artist, landscape architect, gardners, craftspeople, engineers and the industry. What I learned though was that even if you have teams of people working with you, the only thing that really makes it happen is *you* – you must be the driving force behind it, gathering up others and spurring them on, and inspiring confidence and energy." Research Fellow at Cardiff Institute of Higher Education during the work's construction, Gwen Heeney looked in detail at how more commissions could be generated in this country through mutually beneficial relationships between artists and industry, drawing on examples from Europe where artists and craftspeople have always done this.

which the scheme has won, secured a funding package to create a green open space on the derelict area adjacent to the transformed subway.

Similarly, Davis noted a great improvement in the readiness of councillors to include artists in schemes in the county as a result of their experiences with Ridge. He warns, though, "these things are only as good as the last project."

4 • Approaches

Paul Swales   The visual arts is a world without rules, but in operating in the public domain it comes into a world circumscribed by rules, regulations, economics, attitudes, and legislation, where corporate and individual egos are writ large. It is also in a democratic world where politics and a collective voice have sway.

In modern terms 'public art' is a new phenomenon. The term gives no clue to what it might be as it is a contradiction: the private activity of visual enquiry being linked to the collective, the social order and self-negation. Where once there was a coherent society, there is now a pluralistic one without a unifying religion or consensus on social, cultural, political or moral matters. In a very real sense, we have lots of people, interest groups, and communities, but no public.

The public domain forces art to compete with the public culture of mass marketing, television and the myriad of urban or rural distractions whilst attempting to engage an audience with no understanding or knowledge of the contemporary visual arts.

Agencies

Jerry Allen, 'How Art Becomes Public', *Going Public*, Cruikshank and Korza, Arts Extension Service, 1988

There is a national consensus promoted by art organisations and magazines of what contemporary visual arts is. But their understanding isn't the public's understanding of art. To get approval to put art in the public domain, it has been promoted as a way of enhancing well-being in the visual and spiritual poverty of our cities, improving dismal spaces and uplifting bland lives. This can be seen in the work of public art agencies who have "devised numerous approaches that interject largely non-aesthetic content into their art projects", filling the gap between the artist and audience with **administrative** procedures.

Susanna Robinson, 'Making it Work', *Artists Newsletter*, June 1992

A "disappointed and disillusioned" Susanna Robinson complained the "...agency gained a substantial amount of control over the commission before any artists were brought in" and that "client and artist can communicate well with each other, and have an interesting and exciting relationship.... There is no reason why the artist shouldn't also communicate directly with the workforce or bureaucracy... Depending on an interpreter is not going to help the artist's relationship with the public in the long-run, and can be costly and counter-productive both to artist and client."

An analogy with estate agents can be made. They keep seller and buyer apart and produce fanciful details. As their fee is charged on the selling price, it is in their interest to get the best possible price. Similarly, public art agencies act primarily on behalf of their clients, the paying commissioners. There is a case for the introducer to step back and let the relationship develop on terms that suit both parties.

This administrative buffer has been likened to a 'Royal Society for the Protection of Artists', suggesting that practitioners of this mysterious 'art' are sensitive souls requiring 'special' treatment not extended to other professions. This reinforces the view that art is not a part of daily life and is a special treat that does us good. Furthermore it has been remarked that the so-called 'public art' in this country is not very good. But the nature of urban spaces and architecture the artists have to deal with is nothing to write home about either.

Visual artists

The confidence shown by the establishment in a small number of artists to do a good piece and behave themselves at meetings has no effect on the wider constituency of visual artists and the audiences they may be able to develop. The reasons for non-participation by a large proportion of artists are probably more bound-up in attitudes in the arts, than in the real world.

This view is not new. Edward Bruce, pioneer of public art programmes for Roosevelt's 'New Deal' lamented the red-tape and that he had difficulty finding good artists, privately admitting "the honest fact of the situation is that we get no real support from artists." What was true then is true now. If you're in the know, you're on the short-list. Though it's equally true that lack of training in this field has disadvantaged artists who wish to be involved. Not having the knowledge, confidence, training or personal skills to operate in the public domain has not helped artists develop a personal strategy or methodology for dealing with art in public.

R D McKinzie, *The New Deal For Artists*, Princeton University Press, 1973

If one of the aims of artists, makers and art administrators is to increase the contact between individuals and visual arts in daily lives, art in places has a great value, greater than simply ameliorating a dismal space.

John Buckley **and** *Shark.*
Photo: Dave Green

The city council claimed the shark installed in the roof of Bill Heine's terraced house in Oxford in 1986 breached planning regulations. Heine argued "the issue is the freedom of artists to express themselves, an issue that affects not just artists, but everyone in the community." Neighbours expressed support of it – one changing the name of her house to 'Sharkview'. "Everyone expected me to object (but) the shark makes no noise, doesn't smell and isn't on a double yellow line. I think it's great."

Enhancement

The issue of "enhancement" should not be completely dismissed. Bill Heine has to thank the Department of the Environment inspector who upheld his appeal against Oxford City Council planners who wanted the removal of John Buckley's *Untitled 1986 – The Oxford Shark.* The inspector, as reported in *The Planner,* decided "any system of control must make some small space for the dynamic, the unexpected and the downright quirky, or we shall all be the poorer for it... I believe this is one case where a little vision and imagination is appropriate." The junior Planning Minister agreed emphasising that the purpose of planning control was not to enforce "boring and mediocre uniformity" on the built environment. Bill Heine took trouble to carry people with him, attending meetings, writing letters, and discussing art. At the end of the day, the decision was not made on art grounds, but strictly on planning issues and what we can expect in our environment.

Bringing together, directly, artist and 'public' – whether the audience, contractor's workforce or local bureaucracy – is the most effective way of re-establishing links between contemporary art practice and the public. It isn't that architects don't engage artists on building schemes, it's that they often don't know where to find them, or what artists do.

How this link is achieved on a personal basis is a matter for the individual. It can be as simple as the confidence to act and take on issues and concerns surrounding an art for places project, including the multiplicity of rules and regulations that exist in the "real world". Some artists will not be comfortable without a helping hand and training, there are some sharks out there. But in the main, the exotic nature of art draws people in. The architect, planner, designer or site-manager is on a learning curve as well. The process is two-way. Part of the public (the audience) will have a direct, educative contact with art, and the artist becomes well-versed in the arcane languages of planning, architecture and bureaucracy.

Conferences, studies, reviews and awards promoted by arts organisations need to be supplemented by practical training recognised by the Royal Town

Joanna Veevers, **detail of paving scheme design for Don Valley Stadium, Sheffield, in collaboration with an architectural technician. Photo:** the artist

Although not implemented, this is an example of applying normal art concerns to a public arena. The artist, who usually makes small-scale tiles and jewellery, applied her ideas about colour and pattern to an object 50m across.

Planning Institute and Royal Institute of British Architects. If arts bodies are unable to establish professional parity between artists and architects, perhaps artists have a part to play in establishing local connections which will lead to mutual respect and understanding.

At the heart is the production of work – the making of art that has numerous considerations as part of its content, the area where private concerns are pursued within a public framework and what is made, how and why. Again this must be personal choice. The strategies employed will vary from person to person, project to project and site to site, and there is no template that fits every situation and all types of work. Golden rules of 'commissioning' – the artist must be engaged at the earliest opportunity or the artist must be part of the design team – are rules often broken, and not always appropriate to how an individual artist works or wants to work. Just as there are times when a design is initiated by an artist at the start of a building scheme, and others when the artist will appear at the end. This is entirely as it should be. Artists make work in different, personal ways.

American models

R D McKinzie, *The New Deal For Artists*

In the main, art for places in this country has followed American models. They have after all been promoting contemporary artists working in public since Roosevelt's 'New Deal', the 'Works Progress Administration' and their first percent for art programme in 1934. The critical debate about art in places has also largely occurred in America, where working in the public domain is a mainstream activity and not, as in this country, a compromised, marginal area of interest.

Art Journal, USA , winter 1989

An issue of the American magazine *Art Journal* amplified the differing approaches to public art issues. Artists and critics mapped out a broad area of work and approaches to the subject that allows for a

Work in progress on *Walking Women*. Photo: the artist

Commissioned from André Wallace **in a limited competition organised by Speyhawk plc for a Standard Life development at BR/Underground Wimbledon Station and town hall. The 8' high bronze work emerges from two pillars and is approached by steps.**

diversity of professional practice whilst retaining integrity, innovation, and experimentation. The comments may seem contradictory, but are based on personal aesthetics and individual ways of working.

"Although it is at an exploratory stage, public art is treated as if it were a production of fixed strategies and principles... Clearly public art is not public just because it is out of doors, or in some identifiable civic space, or it is something everyone can apprehend; it is public because it is a manifestation of art activities and strategies that take the idea of a public as the genesis and subject for analysis." (Patricia C Phillips)

"If art in the public context does not address the context, then its uniqueness, site to site, becomes obsolete. We would be left with the homogeneity now prevalent in this country, where each city looks like the next." (Andrea Blum)

"In defense of 'plop' art: anything so maligned can't be all bad." (Joyce Kozloff)

"Is it there for mere decoration? If so, what's so mere about decoration?" (George Sugarman)

"The notion that avant-garde art has to be controversial and subversive is an out-dated remnant of modernism. It is now time for art to start functioning again within its social context." (Athena Tacha)

"One of the things that I find most compelling is trying to make a strong visual, physical, and emotional experience accessible to people who aren't necessarily those who go into museums regularly." (Mary Miss)

Approaches

Janet Kardon, Director Institute of Contemporary Art, University of Pennsylvania in *Placemakers*, Fleming and Von Tscharner, Harcourt Brace Jovanovich, 1987

How an art for places project is approached is informed by the artist's individual understanding of their practice and their individual objectives for producing work for a public place. Just as there is a wide spectrum in thinking what the public constitutes, there is also another in thinking what can or should the resulting work be. The conflicting quotes below point to a deep divide, but if artists become more fully engaged with the public there will be times when one approach is more justifiable or personally preferable than another.

"In no other area of art activity does the public's 'right to recognise' the subject, content and meaning of the art work apply with

Mary Miss, *South Cove*, Battery Park, New York 1987. **Photo:** Paul Swales

"This is a remarkable marriage of art, architecture and landscape which seems to accomplish the task of transforming a space into a public place. With its landscaped walkways, lookouts, piers and vistas, it brings to mind the picturesque visions of Frederick Law Olmstead, the designer of Central Park. The work's scattered boulders and lush plantings evoke Japanese gardens whilst the battered wood pilings along their pier recall New York as a port town. The artist and her collaborators have created a total environment which is used by visitors who have no idea they are wandering over a piece of public art." ('What's Missing at Battery Park?')

9 Spaces 9 Trees, Robert Irwin. **Photo:** Paul Swales

The Public Safety Building Plaza in Seattle, USA was a barren, unused public space with police car park beneath. The square is supported by nine columns which were used as starting point. Nine 22' squares were marked out and bordered by 8' high blue coated chain-link fence. In the centre of each is a planter with purple-leafed plum tree and hardy green succulent.

The wide rim on each planter acts as a bench, and on the top of each fence is a light angled at the trees.

such force...There is a basic incompatibility between the concepts of space generated by the modern movement and those invoked by traditional realism...The space of abstraction is a different space. Its gravitational rules, its metaphors, its illusions, and its purities are far from the everyday space in which the realist figure stands...The huge abstract sculpture, which celebrates the fact of art above all else, is a threatening experience for a public who finds it without rationale, motive or beauty. The way the abstract artwork relates to the space of the passer-by is one key to the negative reception that has become a kind of certificate of merit among modern artists."

Robert Irwin, *Being and Circumstance: Notes Toward a Conditional Art*, Lapis Press, 1985

"This idea of mine constitutes a kind of general definition for the 'intention' underwriting the present phenomenon of 'site-art'. This as opposed to the generic label of 'public art', a view which draws no useful

Jennie Moncur **Festival Bridges** at the Gateshead Garden Festival 1990. **Photo:** Paul Swales

British Rail's Community Unit commissioned designs for the repainting of 14 rail bridges on or near the festival site. Other commissions for public and private clients have taken the form of tapestries, carpets, painted textiles and the laser-cut linoleum floor for London's Institute of Contemporary Art.

distinctions from past public practices and presently acts as a kind of populist umbrella under which a general chaos prevails. Everything from the classical aspirations of the historical, moralistic, and heroic object-monument, to the do-good social-political utilitarianism and the free-for-all of freeway wall and subway graffiti, qualify as being 'public'. Much of this activity stems from the misconception that the general estrangement that developed between modern art and the general public is due to art having 'lost its way' and that the problem is solvable, that is, reversible, through the simple reintroduction of old and familiar art forms and good deeds performed in the public place. This view is not justified. One needs simply to consider that too many individual artists from too many separate places, with too many real differences in their backgrounds, values and motives, were engaged in its practice and definitions for the 'history' of modern art to be either accidental or incidental."

Jagonari Mosaic by Meena Thakor. **Photo:** Lloyd Gee

The Jagonari Women's Centre is the first Asian women's resource centre initiated, planned and designed by local Asian women and a women's architects' collective. In the plans was the idea to have something decorative for the front, but lack of finances left a 13' rendered area blank. Seeing the potential, the artist approached the centre to make a mural. Although a planned series of participatory workshops fell through, and the artist went on to produce the mural alone. Made from vitreous tesserae and constructed on brown paper before being glued to the wall in sections, it took three months' part-time work to complete.

Local solution

American models of practice or philosophy are not completely transferable, and in all cases the local solution is more preferable and closer to place, public and politics. The strategy of getting close to the place and the personalities surrounding it – whether architects, community groups or administrators – can have the greatest effect on the work and public, creating that often elusive goal: the sense of place.

In a series of articles in January 1984 by Tim Ostler and Steve Field, *Architects Journal* promoted 'Working with Artists', a how-to-do-it guide, complete with a list of what symbolic functions an artwork could have in different parts of different buildings. One comment seems to have been prophetic. "The emergence of Post-Modernism in both art and architecture might suggest more co-operation in the future. However the reverse may prove true. Although there are some signs of rapprochement between the formal preoccupations of artists and architects, restoring the importance of symbolism, Post Modernism does not question the self-image of the architect as the complete artist. Architects may therefore guard even more jealously the role of the 'creative person' in the design team, and lay claim to any proposed art for the purpose of improving the expressive content of the building."

Architects present a professional face and can be aggrieved when told an artist would 'enhance' their scheme. But to be treated as professional, artists and makers must negotiate and assert their case to be considered equals of architects who consider themselves artists using the built form. Magazines and reviews may show us the great achievements of collaborations between exciting architects and artists, but 99% of the time you will be dealing people who have more modest considerations than making grand architectural statements.

The real world is stacked against contemporary visual arts, and the antipathy towards artists is not simply the result of outside factors. With this in mind it seems paradoxical that when an art for places project is mounted, the degree of interest is enormous, not least because everyone can have an opinion on art, and they have probably not met an artist before.

It is difficult to articulate objections to purely technical or regulated matters. If the guidelines insist on a minimum distance between a playground and a housing area, then that is the distance. Although artists have often resolved physical problems creatively, land reclamation projects for example, where art is concerned the lack of rules or boundaries is one of its greatest assets. Art can become a focus for a number of issues or concerns, either public or private, making visible the invisible ideas, concerns or needs of the artist and audience. Artists who work in the public domain will testify to the public's interest and willingness to discuss art, maybe not within the contemporary-art-gallery-workshop-education-space-context, but on their own territory. The resulting work can carry numerous levels of meaning through materials, form, production methods, content, metaphor etc. It is this ability to effect a transformation of the commonplace in direct communication with others that gives the artist a vital role in the public arena.

Wider context

To operate successfully in a public arena requires specific personal objectives as well as understanding of the wider context of art for places. The objectives may be money (earning a living from your professional

Herbe Garden by Graeme Moore. **Photo:** East Anglian Daily Times

In 1989, for Ipswich Museums and Art Galleries 'Arts in Town' project, Graeme Moore made three landscape works based on his interest in environmental issues and the garden tradition. *Herbe Garden* at Christchurch Park was a pun, the design relating back to the park's mansion. It was intended the works should be permanent, cared for by the Parks Department, but budget restrictions forced the department eventually to 'cut' them all.

practice), learning new skills, working on a larger scale, working with new materials, making new work or re-establishing the link between art and daily life.

Strategies employed vary from project to project and person to person, but common to all is a necessity to

Andy Parkin, Bruce Williams
and Christopher McHugh –
collectively known as Artonic –
contributed to awareness-
raising activities for 'World
AIDS Day' by creating an
animated light display in which
'T' cells from the human blood
stream infected by HIV and
magnified to the 'Nth' degree
were animated to form the
backdrop to the message that
AIDS and HIV are not issues for
someone else to deal with. It
was assisted by Maiden
Outdoor Advertising, Spike and
Red Herring Studios in
Brighton.

communicate ideas, and surely art is a method of communicating ideas. Working with people who are unused to looking at contemporary art, and have no qualms about suggesting alterations, can be challenging: they don't know art's unwritten rules. You will be working in a world where team working and the views of others are used collectively. Alterations occur because consultation and comment from other professionals or public groups is ongoing. The process is lengthy, and your work may only be a small part of a larger scheme, but although you may not be equipped to comment on a highway alignment, you can bet the highway engineer will have an opinion on your work.

Convincing others of your ideas is the dynamic of team working which produces a sense of ownership, and ensures a successful outcome. The communication of information, whether content or techniques employed is the bed-rock of producing art in places. Whether the idea communicated verbally or visually is a personal choice. Some artists are adept at making models, scale drawings and written reports, though talking a client through a project using quick sketches, and material samples is very effective, especially if done in your studio. "I take this, do this, add this bit like that (a bit like the piece in the corner), fasten it together there...." Either way it is a process of building a picture in the client's mind of what the work will be, the ideas, the content, how it relates to the place, and what it might look like, establishing confidence in the client that you can make it, and have considered the problems or benefits associated with the place.

The range of types of work that can be produced for a place is wide. Seattle Arts Commission produced a planning study in 1984 which

'Artwork Network', *A
Planning Study for
Seattle: Art in the
Civic Context,*
Hirschfield and
Rouch, Seattle Arts
Commission, 1984

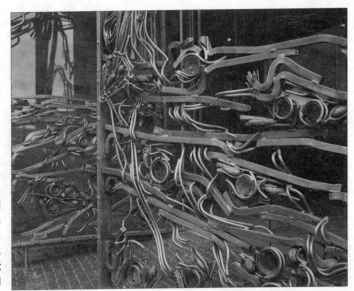

Detail of Michael Johnson's **gates for Birmingham Jewellery Centre. Photo:** Stuart Blackwood

Architect Derek Latham, introduced to the artist's work through the company Omega 2, asked him for proposals for the 19' x 11' gates to the centre for presentation to the development's clients. He worked with the architects to put forward a 'presentation package' which instead of containing predictable 'artist's impressions', used sketches and samples of materials and documentation of previous work to put over how he would approach the commission. As well as the gates, constructed in stainless steel, cast glass and brass, he was commissioned to make a sign bracket, light fittings, handrails, ballustrading and metalwork anchor images to inset into stone slabs. The commission, valued at £28,000 to include 3 tons of material, took twelve weeks to make and install.

Robert Irwin, *Being and Circumstance: Notes Toward a Conditional Art*

usefully examined the scope of work being created. Based on the understanding that the artist alone is not responsible for the appropriateness of artwork and site and that commissioners play a vital role in determining a site, the study looked at the 'Expressive Vocabulary of the Work' ('Abstraction or Representation'), the 'Relationship of the Artwork to the Site' (not related, designed for a generic site and unique to a specific site) and the other issue that helps define a particular work, 'The Relationship of Artwork to its Audience'.

73

Tree by Richard Perry, made in Portland stone 3.5m x 91.5cm, commissioned for the courtyard of Northampton Guildhall Extension by Northampton Borough Council in 1991. **Photo:** the artist

Paul Mason's **tree grilles for Tudor Square, Sheffield. Photo:** Stuart Blackwood

Using a selection of symbols to create a strong visual rhythm seen from any angle, this is an example of a public art puzzle: where does art stop and design begin? An integrated art and design process has created a new city square "not an artwork to be looked at. It is there to be animated, a place to pass through, to sit in in summer. This is how the artwork will be experienced." (David Alston, Deputy Arts Director, Sheffield City.)

Categories

The manner in which the artwork communicates to an audience can be divided into four categories.

- Aesthetic – works are presented to an audience as resolutions of aesthetic issues of interest to the artist. They appeal directly to the viewer's appreciation of the visual form and to their conception of the beautiful.

- Didactic – works meant to instruct or enlighten.

- Functional – works fulfilling a functional purpose, ie a ramp, a bench, or a lamp.

- Symbolic – artworks which attribute meaning or significance to people, objects, events, relationships or goals through the use of symbols or symbolic associations. Within this category lie many 'civic' sculptures.

These building blocks allow a great deal of freedom but, importantly, describe the essential nature of the work to be made. This can be applied to permanent and temporary work. Although individual projects may have a combination of these elements to greater or lesser degrees, by simply stating "I'm going to make you a bench", or "something

Jump Fucker Jump, light projection by Francis Gomila. **Photo:** Gary Kirkham

The imminent demolition of Smethwick's 20-storey Croxall Tower – to be replaced by low-rise housing – was marked by a one-night event of sculpture, video, performance, light and sound in and on the tower by Fine Rats International, artists who specialise in nocturnal events in places of social and architectural significance. Following events in disused factories and an 'art journey' under the M5 motorway, they highlighted Croxall Tower, previously hailed as a brave new solution to the housing problem and now a symbol of inhuman and alienating modernist architecture. Works on eight storeys were created by Francis Gomila, Colin Pearce, Mark Renn and Ivan Smith and guest artists Paul Burwell, Loophole Cinema and Roland Miller.

which symbolises your community", or "a sculpture to contemplate", or "a work about your environment", the scene is set for the next stage of the discussion – how you consider the making processes in relation to the site.

Robert Irwin defined four ways art and site are considered.

- Site dominant – "These works of art are recognised, understood and evaluated by referencing their content, purpose, placement, familiar form, materials, techniques, skills, etc. A Henry Moore would be an example."
- Site adjusted – "Here consideration is given to adjustments of scale, appropriateness, placement, etc. But the work is still made or conceived in the studio."

Pages of the Diary, glazed ceramic panel made in 1989 by Russian artist Anatoly Karmardin from Tver who, as part of East Kilbride Development Corporation's Environmental Art Programme, was invited to make a ceramic panel for the arts centre at Bosfield House. Links with Tver were established several years ago through exchange of artists and exhibitions.

- Site-specific – "Here the sculpture is conceived with the site in mind; the site sets the parameters and is in part the reason for the sculpture. This process takes the initial step towards sculpture's being integrated into its surroundings."
- Site conditioned/determined – "Here the sculptural response draws all of its cues (reasons for being) from its surroundings." Irwin then lists a host of considerations including the weather, people density, sound, movement, qualities of detail, history, etc. In this category the process of recognition and understanding breaks with conventions of artist or style, and crosses the "boundaries of art vis-a-vis architecture, landscape, city planning, utility and so forth."

Milton Estero, 'How Public Art Becomes a Political Hot Potato', *Artnews* 1986, reprinted in *Going Public*

Irwin is one of few artists to have articulated not just questions about art in public, but about the nature of the work in daily life. An article quoted him as saying: "Isn't the art object actually understood as a distinct and special category of thing? What actually happens to what was once distinct and special when we fold it into the fabric of its circumstances? Into our daily lives? Gain or loss? Are you intrigued by the possibilities, or put off by the complexities?" His language may be a bit opaque, but his concern is to open up art in places to all kinds of possibilities and stimuli by presenting a framework to act within.

There is a place for a range of art in the public domain, whether merely decorative, obscurely philosophical, or even quirky. This is not an activity for the few. The confidence to act and to carry through a project that is born out of a private practice is not easy, but when was art easy?

Artists' interests

I have drawn extensively on American quotes because they have a greater body of knowledge and practice gained over a long period of time on the nature of art for places. We are not in America, and we still (just) have a separate culture, but art in places in this country has been stuck in a rut for some time now. The preponderance of celebratory sculpture and brick paving patterns speaks more about the promoters of art in places than the interests of artists. The high-ground though is being reclaimed by artists like Fine Rats International who will respond to invitations to work, but reserve the right to say no and to set the agenda.

America is not a model for everyone, but it has developed a wider and deeper set of objects and strategies that inform 'art in places'. This is summed up in a story about Robert Irwin: "Another time in another city, there was a meeting with some officials. I said about four words and one of them said 'Wait a second. I don't want to know about all that abstract nonsense. As far as I'm concerned, the *Pieta* now that's art. If you can give me the *Pieta*, then we've got a deal.' And I said to him, 'Look, I'll tell you what. I will look at your situation and if I can find anything interesting to do, I'll show it to you. If you're interested, we'll do it. If you're not interested, we won't do it. All bets are off. It won't cost you a thing.' He said, 'Okay, I can understand that.'"

5 • Applications & proposals

Yvonne Deane

The ways in which artists can work in public settings have increased massively in the last decade. Opportunities include working in residencies or to commission in projects which last anything from a few days to several years. Town artists, 'fellows', consultants and animateurs are often included in the staffing structures of local authorities and education institutions. Artists can be found at work in every type of setting, from schools and factories to prisons, from shopping malls and heritage centres to country parks.

But because there are few opportunities for hands-on experience or training and plenty of competition from more experienced artists, moving towards working on a commissioned basis involves an element of trial and error. This is true whether you are developing your own initiatives or entering competitions.

For artists more familiar with studio and gallery environments, taking the plunge can be fraught with difficulties, not least being the 'Catch 22': to get the job you need to demonstrate you know what you are doing.

Despite this drawback, working in public settings offers artists a rewarding, creative and challenging way of developing their art practice. Undoubtedly, an attraction is the potential to earn income from making artwork outside the traditional market place of gallery and exhibition. Many artists see it as more than a way of earning a living. For textile artist Kate Russell, it demonstrates her philosophy. "Art that matters to me 'delights the senses, moves the heart, revives the soul, and offers courage for living'. Since the days of my art education I have held a vision of art that it is not separated from daily life; art that is integrated with the physical, social and cultural fabric of our lives."

The Gift: Imagination and the Erotic Life of Property, Lewis Hyde, Vintage Books, 1979

Whether applying for an advertised commission or trying to realise your own ideas the same principles apply. You need to know how to put together an interesting, attractive and coherent proposal, and to understand what the people and organisations who control and shape opportunities are looking for. The key to success will lie in your ability to put over yourself, your work and your ideas in person and on paper.

A good reason, perhaps for looking through this chapter, absorbing the checklists, and 'taking the plunge'.

Commission structures

Commission and residency opportunities are created:

- by artists for themselves
- by the host or commissioning body
- by specialists or agencies on behalf of another body.

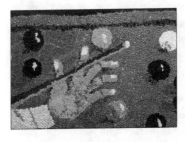

Hooky by Christopher Ross

A detail from a 9' x 6' permanently-sited proggy and hooky hanging *What goes down must come up!*, Ashington Leisure Centre, Northumberland, the result of Kate Russell's residency in 1991.

It is not that one option is preferable to another, but there are definite pros and cons for each. Each method implies a different set of power relationships between artist, agent and commissioner. These can be summarised as the differences between retaining artistic freedom and personal control and dealing with administration and logistical problems.

Artists can be selected for a project:

- by invitation
- by invitation to a short-list – also known as 'limited competition'
- by open competition.

Direct invitations and invited short-lists generally occur when a commissioner has a clear idea of what they want. Invited artists or their work will often be known to the commissioner or to the agents acting for them. For most artists however, their first experience of working to commission will result from applying for an advertised competition.

Artists as initiators

Artists initiate and organise their own commissions for a variety of reasons. Because the majority of advertised opportunities are based in urban areas there is a tendency for artists living in rural areas to rely entirely on their own resources and imagination to create their own work opportunities. For others, organising their own commission means more control in their hands, the chance to identify the site, set the brief, define the aims of the project, and choose the partners to work with.

Detail of the relief carving on Georgia Wright's *Crab and Winkle Line* sea bench at Whitstable. **Photo:** the artist

Whitstable Artists and Musicians Collective played a major part in the development of art in public in Canterbury, instigating the making of five benches on sea themes between 1989 and 1992. Using 100 year-old groyne wood salvaged from the beach during renewal of sea defences, other benches have been made by Nigel Hobbins, William Glanfield, Mark Fuller and Simon Foster-Ogg.

Arts boards for Yorkshire and Humberside, North West, Eastern, South West and Northern England all provide information leaflets for artists on how to carry out residencies and work to commission.

Undoubtedly, there is a bureaucratic tendency to view the development of commissioned work as a job for arts officers and agencies. South West Arts' current funding guidelines state that "priority is given to projects which we have initiated with funding partners and which fulfil our objectives." Other regional arts boards welcome artists' initiatives and several have developed information sheets and advisory structures to facilitate this.

As well as the increasing number of artists who successfully act as their own agents, examples also exist of artist-run agencies. Chrysalis Arts, despite its corporate sounding name, is an informal association of artists held together by Rick Faulkner and Kate Maddison. Acting as promoters for themselves, they also generate opportunities for other artists to work with them on specific commissions. "Working like this allows us to offer commissioners a wide range of skills, expertise and imagination. It also enables us to share experiences and ideas with other practitioners and support less experienced artists."

There are drawbacks to do-it-yourself projects. The administrative and contractual side can be daunting, especially if you are new to to the field. In architecture, it is estimated that only 5% of the architect's time in any project is involved with the creative and imaginative work. Artists working to commission may find this a heavy burden, although Rick Faulkner doesn't. "Perhaps I'm unusual because I have an industrial background, but I see the whole thing as a job. The administrative workload is offset by the opportunity to develop the commission in a way that suits artists as well as commissioners."

In 1992, Edinburgh Sculpture Workshop initiated the *Niches Project* which ran for three months. Ten sculptural assemblies were sited in empty niches in Old Calton Cemetery wall, participants including artists, students and school children using a steel box to bring together everyday objects, sculptures, texts and other material under an overall theme of 'Scottish Culture'. Illustrated is the work made by Edinburgh Sculpture Workshop members.

Benefits include:

- ensuring your work gets public exposure
- exercising control over your own project
- the chance to create challenging work on your own terms
- collaborating with artists of your own choosing
- working with those in the community with whom you have affinity
- working with professionals like architects, designers, engineers
- building on your strengths, interests and expertise
- expanding and improving technical and administrative skills
- expanding artistic possibilities in terms of scale or materials
- getting paid to make new work
- developing work opportunities in your locality.

Disadvantages include:

- operating as a 'small business', dealing with planning, financial control, time-management, public relations
- time taken to work up proposals with no guarantee of success
- lack of access to legal and technical expertise and resources
- time and cost of doing your own negotiation, project management and administration
- dealing with the needs of all involved in the commissioning process
- trouble-shooting if things go wrong.

Note that many of these positives and negatives also apply to making submissions to open competitions.

Open competitions

The growth in open advertised competitions has done much to create opportunities for a greater number of artists to enter the field of art in public. With support from a sympathetic agent, artists can gain invaluable

Developing a private commission

Between Us commissioned from Colin Wilbourn **by Meg Griffin, sited on private land at Gulval, Nr Penzance, Cornwall. Photo:** the artist

Colin Wilbourn's privately commissioned sculpture *Between Us* was generated when a woman visiting her parents in Co Durham visited the Gateshead Garden Festival and saw his work *Shadows of the Past* in the Durham Garden. Impressed by the sculpture's materials – reclaimed elm from Durham woodlands and steel – and its appropriateness to the site, she decided to contact the artist about making a piece in memory of her husband who had died recently. He had been a keen conservationist with a particular love of trees which he had cultivated in a steep-side valley near their house in Penzance.

Getting his address from Durham County Council, she wrote asking him to make a piece from two elms blown down in the 1987 gales.

He visited the site – a valley with two ponds, masses of wildlife and meadow overlooking it and a view across the bay – and showed her examples of his work. They agreed a seat would be the most appropriate thing to make, although because of other commitments, he couldn't start for a while. "We left it there, I came back home with lots of photographs and some rough ideas in my head. A few months later, the idea gelled. I did a drawing and explanation and sent it off. She liked it, so I went down again to check it was feasible, agree a fee and materials costs and when I could do it."

He started two months later, the commissioner providing board and lodging, him working on site twelve hours a day for 25 consecutive days, logging timber, hauling it from the stream, cutting, carving and constructing, laying a concrete foundation and erecting the sculpture.

"She relied on the fact I would be sensitive to her request and make a sound, safe and well-made piece. I trusted she would go ahead with the commission and pay me at the end. We had no contract. I am aware this method is not suitable for other situations, but in this commission it worked because trust was immediately established through the early approaches and planning."

Colin Wilbourn has undertaken commissions for Rowntree Macintosh, the Dean and Chapter of Durham Cathedral, Durham County Council, Scarborough Borough Council and the Northern Centre for Contemporary Art. During 1992/93, he is consultant/artist for the St Peter's Riverside Project in Sunderland.

work experience. A completed commission if well documented and presented makes an important contribution to an artist's CV, and improves their chances of gaining work in the future. Working through an agent, artists are freed from a substantial part of the administrative workload, have access to legal and financial advice and are free to concentrate on the creative and technical aspects of a commission.

Susanna Robinson,
'Making it Work',
Artists Newsletter,
June 1992

Or are they? Artist Susanna Robinson, whilst acknowledging the important role commission agents play in instigating and developing commissions, warns against a naïve assumption that all are competent and supportive. "The agency proved not to have expertise with my particular work. They caused almost £1000 worth of damage to the work in storage. There were almost disastrous results through a last-minute and inadequate lifting process."

A common view is that entering open competitions demands a high investment of time and resources with a slim chance of success. For example, Lynne Gant was one of a short-list of three artists selected from over 160 applicants for a commission at Lancaster Moor Hospital – which leaves the rest with little return for their investment.

Moreover, the mass nature of competitions means that little or no feedback gets back to applicants – even those who reach the first interview stage. Doug Cocker feels strongly about this. "There is seldom any feedback from agencies when you have participated unsuccessfully. I recognise the need for discretion, but artists need to know how they got it wrong in order to learn from the experience."

Not only that but, for those who get onto the short-list – for interviews or for the further designs or maquette stage – the financial rewards are poor. Doug Cocker points out: "Most of the working, planning, and creative thinking goes into this stage of the project, yet as a percentage of the total budget, the design fee is invariably inadequate."

But the time invested in putting a proposal or preliminary designs together – whether for a self-initiated project or in response to a competition brief – need not be wasted altogether if your project doesn't succeed. Proposals for 'projects not yet realised' can be added to your portfolio and shown to potential clients to demonstrate the way you work. Also, they can be revised and submitted to other competitions.

Planned development

Most artists keep their options open, applying for interesting commissions opportunities as they are advertised, ensuring slides and documentation are on indexes and registers and also preparing their own proposals at the same time. An artist has to be clear about what is right for them. Being

Doug Cocker's *Flock*, 14' high in sycamore. Photo: the artist

This was made during a year-long fine art fellowship with Essex County Council and sited at Oaklands Park in the grounds of Chelmsford Museum and Art Gallery.

objective and recognising your own capabilities and limitations enables you to plan and assess the development of your work, and not become worn down by rejection. You'll need to:

- identify your strengths and weaknesses. What are you good at and most interested in doing? What additional skills do you need?
- decide whether you are ready to generate your own work or whether applying to competitions would be better at this stage.
- be realistic. Don't waste energy and resources applying for commissions beyond your capabilities.
- build up your CV by undertaking small-scale commissions or projects.
- build on what you know and what you are good at.

Preparation

"Preparation is more than... arranging dates, times, budgets and materials... it's a consultative process... between independent professionals."
(Residencies in Education)

There is no substitute for doing research at an early stage. Although this is a familiar concept for artists who regularly initiate their own commissions, it also applies when making an application for a commission. The more work done identifying and costing materials, checking technical information and working out detailed time-scales and budgets, the more confident you will be about the proposal.

Never under-estimate the practical considerations. A budget with ridiculously low costs is as likely to lose you the work as one which is over the top. And if a 'bargain basement' price does get you the job, and then you realise it has been under-costed, you have the problem of how to carry it out without loss of quality or without a fee for yourself. If you have to abandon the commission because the price was fixed too low, not only do you lose face, but the commissioner may be disinclined to work with artists in the future.

Checklist

- For competition submissions, stick closely to the brief. Make a site visit where possible and ask for more information if needed.
- Find out as much as possible about the site and its context – who uses it, why and how.
- Research policy and criteria of potential funders. Ring to get up-to-date information before preparing applications.
- When initiating a project, instigate early informal discussions with potential funders or commission partners by sending a brief letter followed by a telephone call.
- Don't make contact until you've done enough background work to make the project sound interesting and viable. Be sure you can describe how the project will benefit all involved with it.
- If you need to discuss an outline proposal with someone with more experience, some regional arts boards run one-to-one surgeries to talk through projects at an early stage.

Principles

The Arts Council's Education Department produces *Partners*, a fact pack including a sample contract and checklist of questions which will help artists to decide whether they should look for opportunities in educational settings.

Whether making a proposal or an application, the same principles apply. Keep the paperwork 'short and sweet'. Think about how it will come over to the people who look at it. Not everyone who reads it will be an expert in contemporary art and its unique terminology, so avoid or explain artworld jargon.

Thinking about how the information will be interpreted by whoever will read it enables you to tailor the description of your work and your working methods to the best advantage. Put yourself in their shoes, what would you want to know? What would make the proposal come to life?

Contents checklist:

- covering letter on one side of an A4 sheet with a concise summary of your proposal
- list of contents in order
- for a competition application, a description of the artistic concept to accompany the designs or visual material
- for your own initiative, the project proposal
- brief, coherent artist's statement
- up-to-date CV adjusted to the particular circumstances of the application

Billboard by Sarah Quick.

As part of the 1992 International Women's Festival, members of Bristol Women's Photography Group with sponsorship from Mills and Allen, funding from Bristol City Council and use of resources at Arnolfini, made images using massive black and white photo-copied enlargements of A3 originals for three 10' x 20' billboards. Karen Antonelli, Jan Ceravalo, Liz Milner, Jan Pemberton, Sarah Quick and Alison Wills **each had a week's showing.**

- list of the designs or visuals enclosed with titles, medium, sizes, dates
- if available, extracts from good press coverage of previous work
- pertinent extracts of descriptions of previous projects
- publicity brochure if available.

Quality control

Don't assume the originality and relevance of the creative aspects of your work carry the most weight. There are other key factors which affect how an application or proposal will be received. The care and thought put into written and supporting materials will give the people reading it confidence in your professionalism and organisational abilities.

Remember also that your application will generally be photocopied several times and that designs, artwork and slides, because they will need to be handled throughout the selection processes, need to be protected from finger prints and accidental damage.

Artists' applications often fall at the first fence because of poor-quality written or visual material. Rick Faulkner is critical of the lack of practical training in some institutions at undergraduate level "Artists need to be enabled to adopt a more professional approach. Poor presentation will not do their work justice, no matter how innovative their ideas."

To overcome this, Public Arts in Wakefield – like most professional agencies – automatically provides guidelines for artists on making submissions. Director Graham Roberts says that they "have learned through experience to get artists to standardise what they send. This is partly to help with administration and photocopying but, more importantly,

Responding to a brief

In 1992, Trafford Metropolitan Borough Council allocated £20,000 to improve the viewing area in Davyhulme Park within a larger refurbishment scheme.

The commission brief stated the need to allow for disabled access, the site's function as a vantage point over formal gardens and ponds, and the variety of public using the park. The work was required to be easy to maintain, be safe and durable and built to last. Community consultation and involvement was also expected. Proposals to undertake the commission had to include:

- design drawings – a number of options if preferred.

- information about fabrication – type of materials to be used, means of attachment.

- how on-site work would be carried out, eg how much of it done by contractors other than the artist/company.

- whether it was preferred to undertake the whole job or to work with council contractors.

- specific areas where there is a need for liaison with council landscape architects.

- preliminary breakdown of costs, with consideration given to the balance between production costs and installation of artworks and costs of hard landscaping/structural work identified as part of the refurbishment.

- information about the nature and cost of community consultation for which there is a separate budget.

Chrysalis Arts' 16-page full-colour proposal, spiral bound with encapsulated colour cover offered two approaches to the brief. Option 1 was to work with the existing structure, replacing the railings, adding seating and a path/access ramp, with community input to the design. Option 2 was to demolish the existing structure, re-landscape the area adding disabled access ramp, mosaic paving, timber seating, steel railings, panels and archways, all with community design input.

The proposal illustrated Option 1 using a colour photo-copy of the site with a pull-down tab revealing the suggested alterations. In more detail, it showed how railings and brickwork could be integrated, with community workshops generating designs for steel panels. Option 2 was illustrated using a mixture of coloured line drawings and photographs of previous or similar work.

One theme suggested, 'Cliff, cove, cormorant and cod', involved a domed flat circular mosaic sea bed, cormorant railing

*Chrysalis Arts' **Cormorant post in the 'Cliff, cove, cormorant and cod'** concept.*

Completed work by Chrysalis Arts **at Davyhulme Park.**
Photo: Paul Herrmann

posts, wave designs for railings and seats and a cove created by rocks carved with fossil designs for the site's archway. Another possible theme was 'Curves and colour', with blue glass mosaic tiles, heavy wooden seating and circular community-designed panels in the railings.

For Option 2, with the existing structure demolished and a new mound created, a central community mosaic was proposed, linked with the access ramp, community design seat ends, circular seating and steel decorative panels. (A subsequent survey of the existing structure showed that repair would probably swallow all the budget and to create an arts input required either an increased budget or the structure to be demolished.)

Completed during March and April, the council chose Option 2, and asked for a further set of design ideas based on replacing the structure with a disabled access mound for which the landscape department had already done some sketch designs. The theme of the central circular mosaic became 'time and the seasons', 14 school and community groups as well as families and individuals contributing to its design and making. The theme for ten steel panels around the seating area was the 'natural and urban environment underground', with Flixton High School creating templates for fabrication in steel by blacksmiths.

The overall budget, including community involvement and re-landscaping, was £25,000, small for the scale of the commission. Although this restricted the scope of design work, the results were of good quality and well received by council and the public.

The 30' Forbury Gardens lion,
wrapped and bar-coded,
questioning the relationship
between price and value was
proposed by Jenny Eadon and
Arthur op den Brouw for the
artist-run Reading Visual Arts
Week in 1992. Wrapping took
five people nine hours
although it was vandalised and
burned down three days later.

to make sure that everyone's work is represented on a par with the others."

Submissions should be:

- typed – or at least legibly handwritten
- concise, interesting and without art jargon
- clean
- attractive but not over designed
- easy to photocopy – A4 or A3, in black or dark blue ink
- easy to handle – in a self-contained plastic folder for example

Remember to:

- put your name on each page and all contents
- number the pages
- keep copies of everything including all visuals
- never send originals unless specifically requested, in which case insure them against loss or damage
- for competitions, never send more than is asked for.

What is a proposal?

The aim of a proposal is to give a brief and enticing introduction to a project concept. As it is your opportunity to capture the imagination and interest of future partners and employers, it needs to anticipate and answer all of the initial questions the recipient of the proposal is likely to have about the project.

- Who is involved?
- What is the project about and what will the end result be?
- When will it happen?
- Where will it take place?
- Who will benefit from it?
- Why is it of interest?
- How can it be achieved?

The detailed explanation should cover the headings and points listed below.

Aims

- How the project will benefit you, the community, others who will be involved.

- Outcome of the project – eg temporary or permanent art work, environmental improvement, community participation.

Concept

- Artwork, medium, size, subject, although if an early approach, don't be too specific, refer to relevant examples from your own or other people's work.
- Site's geography, history, context, function, users, problems, etc.
- How the community will be consulted and involved.
- Design ideas or other visual material.
- Support for the proposal from people who will be involved – councillors, community leaders, funders, sponsors, etc.

Production

- Production process and likely time-scale to complete the project.
- Estimated costs and possible sources of income if known.
- Contractual issues which need to be agreed – ownership, maintenance, copyright, insurance, responsibilities,etc.

Curriculum vitae

CVs are an important application tool. Not just a chronological list of education and qualifications, a CV should give a rounded picture of you as an interesting and unique individual, suited and well-qualified to undertake the work for which you are applying. Don't feel embarrassed to expand and embellish areas you feel are important and to omit the irrelevant. Make sure your CV is:

- up-to-date
- adjusted to fit the work for which you are applying
- descriptive rather than a simple list
- typed and well-presented.

Supporting material

Most applications offer some room for the inclusion of 'supporting material'. This mysterious category is an opportunity to include photocopies of good press coverage, extracts from catalogues or critical reviews, selected paragraphs of previous project reports, as well as slides, photographs and even video records of your work.

If you don't have any, improvise. Previous commissioners or clients may be willing to write in support of your work, or you could write your own brief summary of recent successful projects.

Visual material

Pay particular attention to the visual material included. Make sure it accurately represents your work and shows it in the best possible light. If it doesn't, you will be doing yourself a great disservice.

Stick to competition guidelines, which usually specify whether slides or photographs are required, and how many are needed. Visual material must be:

- in focus, correctly lit and showing nothing other than your work
- labelled with your name, title, date, medium
- suitably packaged to go through the post and easy to view – an A4 plastic slide holder is best
- relevant to the application
- of good examples of your work.

Portfolio

The same principles of care and attention to detail also apply to your portfolio. You need to consider how its contents are going to be presented and displayed to those making the selection. If you haven't been told, ask. If the folio has to be left behind, it is especially important to provide a descriptive list of what it contains, just in case anything goes astray.

Check the brief for specific requests and constraints on what to send. Don't include your life's work, be selective. A few good quality pieces are preferable to a large quantity of middling works. Selectors may only get as little as 15 minutes to look at a portfolio. Before delivering a portfolio, check:

- is it easy to flick through?
- is everything labelled?
- is it clean and tidy?

Making designs work

No-one can provide a formula that will ensure success. Nothing can compensate for a poor design concept, lack of originality or failure to address the brief. The following list aims to help you make the best of your opportunities and put your designs and maquettes in the best possible light.

- Check the brief for presentation requirements.

Example of a brief

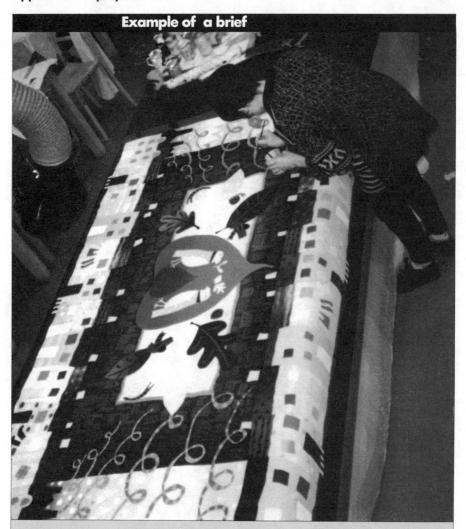

Usha Mahenthiralingam **working on the St Luke's Hospital textile commission. Photo:** Caring Arts

The brief for this commission for the main staircase at St Luke's Hospital in Bradford organised by Caring Arts said: "As part of the major building programme, Caring Arts wishes to commission a textile artist to design and produce a wall-hung work measuring 1800x2350mm for the main staircase, in an area of the hospital that will principally accommodate adult and child out-patient departments, rehabilitation, dentistry, plastic surgery, special treatment clinics and hospital administration.

"The staircase, which leads to all medical and surgical wards, is fully enclosed with no natural light, illumination being by spot or flood lights. A handrail system is fixed to all walls. To comply with fire resistant regulations, it is essential the work is 'finished' according to standard specification. Careful consideration must also be given to the future cleaning of all materials used.

"The artist will work in consultation with the hospital community and Caring Arts to ensure the work is suitable for the site and that it reflects the historical and cultural conditions of patients, visitors and staff.

"Following consultation, the artist will present a minimum of three concept ideas to the commissioning panel, one of which will be selected for full development and production. The artist will be expected to supply the completed textile work by November 1991.

"The commission is sponsored by Save and Prosper Educational Trust. A commission fee of £2000 inclusive of materials is offered and there is an additional expenses budget of £150."

- Keep designs and maquettes clean.
- Make sure they are sturdy and will stand up to repeated handling.
- Include a list of contents with descriptions.

Other methods which may help set your designs apart from the rest include using a video, collage, photo-montage or working model. But if you decide to present technical drawings you may need to get professional help producing them. Artists often include small samples of the actual materials to be used to help put their concept over.

What is a brief?

The term 'brief' comprises a set of instructions and definitions which all parties use as a guide to their responsibilities during the course of a project. It differs from a contract because it is more descriptive, provides contextual information about the history of the site, the aims of the host organisation or specific technical requirements for a commissioned artwork. It may be referred to in the contract and become part of the legal agreement with the commissioner. The brief provides you, the commissioner and anyone else involved with a constant point of reference. If necessary, it also provides the material to deal with legal disputes. It is important to get the brief right.

Creating your own brief

For artists' own initiatives the basis of the brief is your proposal to the commissioner. In effect, you are suggesting that through discussion, you mutually develop your proposal into a workable brief for a commission. As negotiations progress, the project concept will inevitably change from the initial outline. Costings and time-scale will become clearer and the scale and scope of the commission will be agreed. It is essential that before beginning to make the work, all agreements and decisions about the project are finalised in writing and supported by a written contract or letter of agreement.

Competition briefs

An open competition usually has an outline brief for the project circulated with details of how to enter. If you get through to the next stage, there will usually be a more detailed version of it, along with an outline contract, describing requirements for designs and maquettes. Finally, once selected, you will get a full brief confirming the exact nature of the commissioned work linked to a contract.

One reservation artists have about competitions is the notion of artistic compromise, feeling that often the commission brief is set too early, too tightly, and without input from the artist. Rick Faulkner feels that "artists have to be involved in the process as early as possible. Initiating your own commissions is one way of achieving this but, even when applying for open competitions, there is always room for renegotiation. In my experience, commissioners, like architects and landscape architects, are sympathetic to the idea of change and redefinition."

Changing the Brief

No brief should be seen as a holy writ – at least not when first presented to you. Rick Faulkner again: "The brief and end solution should reflect the unique circumstances of the commission. Just because you did a good mosaic path last time doesn't mean you only do mosaic paths. Experienced artists know that they can question a brief that imposes a particular artistic solution, but for less experienced artists, the brief can seem inflexible."

Development of the brief is part of the process of recruitment, selection, appointment and 'briefing' of selected artists. This process should involve the discussion, negotiation and agreement of every aspect of the commission.

'Agreement' is absolutely essential. It is vital that all parties – not just artist and agent – agree the brief. Otherwise, no matter how well the artist fulfils the brief, they may well face rejection somewhere along the line: "We thought everyone knew the work had to be... figurative... in brick... no more than 30" high."

In the period of negotiation, between being offered the commission and signing the contract, the artist gains a clear understanding of everyone's needs and aspirations, uncovers any hidden agenda, and sees where the commissioner can be encouraged to be more adventurous and flexible with the ideas they have for the project.

What goes in a brief?

A finalised brief covers most or all of the following points:

"...don't make the brief too rigid. Leave enough scope for an artist or craftsperson to propose inventive solutions of their own." (Advice to commissioners in *Art and Craft Works*)

- parties involved
- what is required from the artist
- why the project is happening
- location or suggested location of artwork
- possible themes or content
- selection procedures for each stage of a competition
- selectors
- historical, cultural and social factors surrounding the site – usage, community languages and ethnic diversity

Iain Brady with fibreglass angler fish and gannet letterbox sited near the Butt of Lewis. Photo: Sam Maynard

In 1991, An Lanntair Arts Centre, Stornaway introduced 'public art' to the Western Isles in a practical, accessible and appealing form, drawing attention to the importance of the postal service and communication. Artists Reinhard Behrens, Iain Brady, Stephen Dilworth, Louise Scullion and George Wyllie were commissioned to make free-standing letter boxes for siting outside rural households in Lewis and Harris, making an informal sculpture trail. Postcards are published to publicise it.

- present function of the site – landmarks, noise levels, light levels, scale, permanence, durability
- budget and fees available for each stage of the commission
- time-scale and deadlines if possible
- administrative support, steering groups and liaison points
- resources available – studio, accommodation, travel expenses, etc
- how and in what form applications should be made
- responsibilities for site preparation, transport of works, safety, insurance, etc
- constraints on architectural styles or types of materials.

Contract

The most effect way of sealing agreement of a brief is to draw up a contract, a legally binding document which protects your interests. As well as the above points, it should cover planning consents and other permissions likely to be needed, cut off clauses and arbitration procedures and details of maintenance, copyright and ownership. A commission contract checklist is contained in *Making Ways* (see Further Reading) and a model commission contract will be available from AN Publications as a *Fact Pack* in 1993.

Journey, an environmental artwork about travel and time at Manchester's Piccadilly Station. **Photo:** Partnership Arts

Commissioned by Central Manchester Development Corporation from Partnership Arts, artists Travey Cartledge, Diane Gorvin **and** Phil Bews **with** Terry Eaton **as Project Leader** produced three large bronze reliefs, a variable light work, floorscape, paving, floodlighting and planting as part of a major refurbishment of the station's London Road entrance.

Get it in writing

If no one else proposes to put the brief or contract in writing – you must. Take nothing for granted! Never assume you can trust somebody to keep their word, or that someone else is working for your best interests. They may think they have negotiated a good deal for you, but can you be sure they have covered all the angles? A safeguard is to keep your own notes of all discussions, to maintain a diary of work and events for the duration of a commission and confirm significant changes to an agreed brief in writing, for example, "Dear Joanne, thanks for agreeing to move the submission date to 15 July...."

Rejection or success

Feedback may be hard to get but it is always worth asking for it. Otherwise, how else will you know why you lost the commission, or indeed why you got it? Feedback, however painful the idea of rejection, helps you learn from experience and adjust your approach next time.

There is no easy way to cope with rejection, but conversely, success is also difficult to handle. You may have been offered a commission – but it now seems it will be a nightmare of hidden agendas and conflicting interests, the pay is lousy and nobody has thought about copyright, ownership or maintenance.

Experienced artists may recognise the danger signals and have the courage to call it off. But for artists keen to break into the field, any opportunity may seem better than nothing. Rather than saying 'no', you should feel able to look again at the brief and renegotiate the terms in detail before contracts are exchanged.

Working successfully in the field of art in public involves artists in developing confidence in their own potential and the ability to assert themselves as professional partners in the commissioning process, whilst at the same time retaining the integrity of their ideas.

6 • Working methods

Jeni Walwin This chapter, focusing on collaborations, looks at ways artists work with other people or organisations to achieve specific aims for a work. It investigates the nature of relationships between artists, professionals and practitioners in other skill areas as well as how they work with other artists. These relationships are largely determined by the context in which the art work is intended to be seen. For almost every work of art made for a public site in the UK some form of collaboration is necessary. Common collaborators for artists include architects, planners, engineers, arts programmes, public art agents, community organisations, local authorities and the education sector.

Subversion

Of course there are exceptions. Hit-and-run projects, often the result of intentionally subversive activity, offer no prospect of collaboration nor indeed should they, for implicit in such work is the need to remain outside formal frameworks and to make no concession to the compromises collaborations usually require. Public funding for Ddart – a performance group co-founded by Dennis de Groot – was removed after an episode in 1976. Ddart were supported by the Arts Council to make *The Circular Walk*, a work entailing walking the boundaries of East Anglia linked by a pole on their heads. In spite of the appropriateness of the performance, much adverse publicity was generated, particularly in the tabloid press. The ripple effect on support and funding for this seemingly controversial area of work lasted for years. The company disbanded but de Groot continued without funding to make unannounced performances in Bedford every Saturday afternoon, the site selected by a pin prick on a map. There was no planning, record, documentation or publicity. The audience had no expectation of the work but were interrupted by it whilst doing their Saturday shopping. There was no feedback or analysis of the

See also
Confrontations
catalogue, Laing Art
Gallery, 1987

success or failure of these events, but for a brief period these performances became part of the backdrop of Bedford's shopping experience.

Sadly this way of working has virtually disappeared from the current contemporary art scene in the UK, though there is evidence of it elsewhere. This approach represented a raw, honest and often deeply personal approach to the idea of making work for a new audience. As soon as art made for public contexts becomes part of a programme, scheme or strategy, however well-intentioned that development, work will inevitably be shaped to fit those circumstances. It is not that the challenge of the work is necessarily diminished, just that it becomes 'packaged' in a particular way, influenced by policies and available funds. The hit-and-run approach is no longer so attractive to artists, firstly because temporary intervention has become a recognised art practice and is accommodated in mainstream contexts, secondly because its confrontational nature resulted in some tricky legal and financial responsibilities which artists hoped to avoid, and lastly – most crucially – because the working method rarely generated financial reward for the artist.

Blurring distinctions

Returning to collaborations, there are obvious benefits from working with others on a project. It can be financially efficient, offer opportunities for creating a dialogue with a new public and often requires skill sharing which creates informal training experiences. It also contributes to a blurring of distinctions between practitioners with different areas of specialism, offering new parameters and challenges for artists and inspiring different directions in their work.

As it would be over-ambitious to tackle the entire range of collaborations here, this chapter focuses on approaches to making art in ways which are less well-documented, which result in different kinds of collaborations for artists, and impose a variety of working methods.

The first considers the role of temporary works within the field: who supports them, how are they produced and what can they contribute to the cultural vitality of a place which a permanent object may be less able to do? The second investigates 'invisible collaborations' where the artist's contribution cannot immediately be identified visually but where there is real recognition of an artist's role. Thirdly I looked at some instances where art has been embraced as a useful device within a non-art venture, to see at what point art practice – as opposed to any other – was considered to be helpful in realising aims and ambitions far removed from conventional art development.

Transient Works

Part of *Flying Costumes, Floating Tombs* performance on Arnolfini's quayside, 1991.
Photo: Diane Warden

Integrating contemporary and traditional aspects of festival arts, costume, dance, music and theatre, Keith Khan worked with artists, assistants and schools to make sculptures, costumes and banners. A dance company, musicians, artists, performers and others created a series of choreographed dance and water sequences whilst sculptures suspended from cranes unfolded to reveal dancers, fireworks and music. Costumes, described as body architecture, were designed to extend the body's lines into the surrounding space.

For artist and collaborator there are several appealing aspects to making temporary rather than permanent works. There is often more flexibility and there are fewer legal restrictions and permissions required. Works expected to survive centuries bring with them limitations in material and acceptability and there is a sense that, if it must last forever, it must live up to certain formal and technical expectations. Kate Maddison of Chrysalis Arts believes it possible to be more experimental in temporary projects, and new skills and ways of working are more easily integrated.

Activity of the ephemeral sort can also support permanent objects either by generating interest in an idea for a longer-term commitment or celebrating a permanent building or feature. The two are not mutually exclusive and can be beneficial in reverse. For example, at Broadgate in London, home for 25,000 office workers, siting several major public sculptures within a dramatic architectural environment sets the scene and gives an artistic context for the lunchtime arts events programme.

Conversely there are examples where temporary events have established good community involvement in public art. Stockton Riverside Festival was already an annual feature of the town's calendar when the council invited Chrysalis Arts to co-ordinate the community pageant in 1990. With a total budget of £12,000 for a month of intensive production, artists with a range of skills worked with 30 community centres to create a procession on the theme of gardens. Their finale for the festival – designed by Janet Hodgson and Peter Hatton – has subsequently gained a reputation far beyond the event. Such was the success of Chrysalis' contribution they have been invited back for two subsequent years, although in 1992, half the budget was devolved to a community committee in the hope that in future the town will generate its own celebratory arts activity. If this is achieved Chrysalis feel their removal from it will be a sign of its success. Although Kate Maddison considers it is easier to get a community involved in a project that will be permanent and where there is a visible record of its contribution, if a temporary work celebrates something people feel for strongly, there is real enthusiasm for participation.

Bastille Dances, Cherbourg June 1989 by Station House Opera. **Photo:** Bob van Dantzig

Created with 8000 concrete blocks to celebrate the 1989 French Bicentenary, the work was commissioned by the Theatre de Cherbourg and premiered at the Gare Maritime. It was subsequently performed at the London International Festival of Theatre on London's South Bank, Amsterdam Zomerfestijn, Szene Festival Saltsburg and the Festival de Tardor de Barcelona. It received funding from the Arts Council, British Council and ONDA France.

Reservations

This enthusiasm was distinctly absent from some community members when the proposal to bring Miralda's 'Honeymoon Project' to Birmingham was first mooted. In spite of initial reservations from some artists and groups, several hundred people from all sectors of the community subsequently became involved. Conceived in 1986 by Catalan artist Antoni Miralda, the 'Groom' is the 60m high *Columbus* statue in Barcelona and the 'Bride' New York's *Statue of Liberty*. The celebration of their nuptials has been the focus for spectacular events in eight cities round the world. Birmingham's ceremonial procession and related exhibitions and workshops represent an unique example in this country of an international project making direct local connections.

This ambitious and impressive project embracing artists, craftspeople, musicians and filmmakers involved schoolchildren and the elderly, bringing together amateurs and professionals with a wide range of non-arts skills. There was a place in the project for individuals and for large groups of people; each discovering the most effective and appropriate contribution they could make to an idea conceived by Miralda after a visit to the city in 1990. Weddings are a subject on which most people have views or experience. For this project, which explored the symbolism of monuments and wedding rituals in different cultures, the UK's contribution was an eternity ring (inspired by Birmingham's historic and flourishing jewellery quarter) made to the scale of Liberty's finger and incorporating twelve 'diamonds' symbolising members of the European Community. After Birmingham's grand public ceremony it went to New York for the 1992 'Nuptial Event'.

A video of the final procession by Anne Parouty is available from Ikon Gallery.

Citing the long-term benefits of the project, Birmingham City Council's Director of Arts and Recreation says it has given confidence

The 'Honeymoon Project', initiated by Ikon's Elizabeth Macgregor and funded mainly by Birmingham City Council with financial support from West Midlands Arts, the Arts Council and Visiting Arts, was organised by Birmingham City Council and Ikon Gallery in association with Public Art Commissions Agency.

to local groups who had had little experience of working together and no opportunity to work with an artist of international standing.and gave several people a chance to make work in new ways. West Midlands artist Jane Kelly collaborated with Hattie Coppard on the production of the barge which carried the ring up the canal to the Convention Centre, this giving her opportunity to develop ideas on the social history of weddings previously explored in her MA thesis and in her studio practice. She recognised the need to be clear and convincing in her approach to the barge, appreciating the ambiguity between celebration and lament implicit in the Columbus story, and the dynamic tension between a professional artist wishing to make an individual contribution to the overall project locally and the demands of lead artist Antoni Miralda.

That Birmingham chose to spend some of its allocated one percent of the International Convention Centre building cost on such an ambitious but temporary project is laudable. The ring, carried across continents, will form part of other Honeymoon celebrations and Birmingham's enlightened support to this form of art in public will be recognised and valued.

Invisible collaborations

Collaboration between architect and artist is well documented. Historically, it has provided a natural way of working which has continued in other European countries. The French Beaux Arts System traditionally mixes architecture, painting and sculpture, but since the middle of the nineteenth century in Britain, the training of artists and architects has been separate. There have, however, been repeated attempts to bring artists back together here. The 1951 Festival of Britain demonstrated amongst other things that artists and architects could work to produce an aesthetic unity. Following the example of the rebuilding of Coventry Cathedral, several major public buildings of the '50s and '60s enlisted artists to achieve their particular vision. In the last 30 years there have also been good examples of collaborations but for reasons of economics, the law and training – which militate against a more open approach to the built environment – such examples are few.

'Working with Architects', *Artists Newsletter*, January 1991

Andrew Bradford maintains the real reason artists get squeezed out when it comes to building is because of litigation. Architects, now liable for building defects even after death, are pressurised to ensure contracts and criteria are adhered to.

The 1982 ICA conference on art and architecture acted as a catalyst to form the Art and Architecture Group, with aims to "to re-establish a platform for active collaboration between architects, craftspeople, planners, the building industry and patrons of the arts, in sympathy with the needs of the public." Edinburgh then took the lead in implementing a one percent for art policy and the city expects to commission many artworks by 1993.

Critics of percent for art claim that developers will become arbiters of public taste. This has already been demonstrated at Broadgate, where Chief Executive of Stanhope Properties Stuart Lipton has been influential in the choice of artworks sited. Although this has benefits in that a passionate and visionary view of what is possible coupled with an ability to finance the detail of such a project inevitably results in a challenging set of work, it becomes a problem if it is the major form of patronage for art in public. There still needs to be a range of methods for supporting work and enabling other interest groups to commission work to fit their particular needs, so that the dynamic of art for places is maintained.

Still missing from this equation is the sense of real conceptual collaboration between artist and architect at the ideas stage of building development. A working method that does not distinguish between a building's structural function and its visual appearance and yet which retains the artist's central place in a team is still a rarity here.

Few architects have worked with artists to a degree where it is impossible to distinguish between the contribution made by architect or artist. Calling these moments 'invisible collaborations' implies a strength of mutual collaboration where one skill doesn't dominate others.

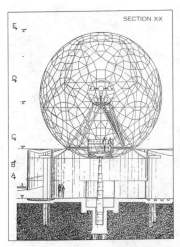

SECTION X-X

Design for the Dubai monument,*The Pearl of the Gulf,* a collaborative project led by architect Ian Ritchie

The central symbol of this building, the 17m diameter 'pearl' is "composed of a double curvature glass skin, whose surface, translucency and 'depth' have been researched to create that ephemeral quality of lustre associated with pearls. The spherical geometry of the glass panels and stainless steel structure is unique and was developed especially for the project, as too is the 'phantom' glass fixing enabling the structure and glass skin to move independently from each other in the harsh environment of the Middle East."

Drawing for *Cascade Amulaire* created by Ian Ritchie and associates for **Parc de la Villette Science Museum, Paris.**

Creating teams

Ian Ritchie, an architect with practices in both London and Paris does not employ a permanent mixed discipline team, but brings in engineers, landscape designers, artists, poets and scientists at the early stages of a project. This working method requires some openness from client and collaborators. Individual fees are negotiated in proportion to the contribution each makes to the project. In some cases, as with the Dubai monument *The Pearl of the Gulf*, special companies are formed. This project included geometry from Ensor Holiday and Keith Laws, visual concept and museum programme from Jean-Louis Lhermitte and architectural design from Ian Ritchie.

It is usual in these situations for the architect to take responsibility for professional indemnity – it is only in France that Ritchie has found it possible to share liability with other collaborators.

Likewise the French seem more able to cope with open collaboration, possibly because artists and scientists are generally held in greater respect across the channel.

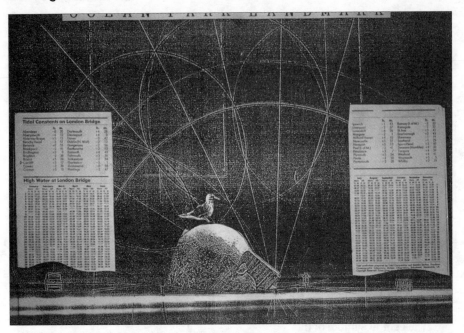

Photo-montage
by Francis Gomila
and Ian Ritchie **for
a landmark for
Cardiff Bay.**
Photo: Francis
Gomila

'Cultural Bridgework',
Murray Fraser,
Building Design,
December 1988

"Only there has Ritchie been able to work closely with artists and engineering companies to produce that combination of science, technology, and art which he felt was essential to make hi-tech real architecture and not mere image-mongering."

A good example was the design for a communications monument for France to give the people of Japan in celebration of the 200th anniversary of the French Revolution and the 100th anniversary of the gift of the *Statue of Liberty* to the American People. *Poesis Generator*, 365m in diameter, 'levitated' by 40 sq m of supermagnets straddling three summits on the site, was restrained by small diameter titanium rods. Contributors to the design team included artist Jean-Louis Lhermitte, graphic artist Guihelm Pratz and engineer Peter Rice.

Will Alsop, another British architect, has often worked with artists, and most regularly with Bruce McLean. He believes they maintain a continuing 'invisible' relationship, constantly collaborating on thoughts, ideas and research in the expectation they will be applied to future projects. In their proposal for the redesign of the centre of Berlin placed fourth in the competition, their collaboration has become most naturally enmeshed. The overall plan appears to be one brightly coloured interlocking sculpture with its own in-built kinetics. The internal and external spaces change with the seasons. "In winter the buildings

One of the Alsop/Stormer coloured drawings for Potzdamer Platz, Berlin. Photo: Alsop/Stormer

The way colour is applied to the buildings is similar to a Bruce McLean painting. It flows enthusiastically through one form and some way across another. Even the green of the tree planting takes on a painterly element in its cross-hatching movement through the squares.

'Berlin Notes', *City of Objects: Designs on Berlin*, Alsop, McLean and Stormer, London Architectural Press, 1992

are the streets... offering protection... and a level of comfort... In summer the parkland is used as the streets... these spaces can provide for performances and exhibitions. They... become an indeterminate theatre.... In spring and autumn the whole area of interiors and exteriors is unified into a whole." The colours of each building sing out in expectation of their use, for example the street of dance and film housing three new cinemas as a permanent home for the Berlin Film Festival is electric blue.

Artist's initiative

Light Year, an installation by sculptor Peter Fink and performance artist Anne Bean with laser designer Martyn Butler on Canary Wharf's Cesar Pelli Tower from December 29, 1991 to January 15, 1992. Photo: Peter Fink

Development of this project – which used a skyscraper as an easel supporting a huge kinetic sculpture visible for over 40km – started in February 1991 and involved negotiations with statutory bodies including the Civil Aviation Authority and London's airports. One of the challenges was to make the tower's height appear insignificant. This was realised through choreographing two kilometre high beams of light above the tower with up to 40 kilometre long laser beams emanating horizontally. A vertical intelligent searchlight display (based on 14 STX 4KW Xenon lights) was placed on external ledges of Levels 6 and 47 of the tower, synchronisation achieved by a data network involving 2km of cable linking the lights to the computer control on the 48th floor. The display used four 5-watt argon lasers radiating north, south, east and west, with a large-frame 25-watt laser providing a westward display to the city. To complement the monumentality of the searchlights and lasers, corners of the building were illuminated with coloured beams to create the appearance of a steeply rising, ever-changing 50-floor high neon sculpture with a highly visible count-down display to herald 1992. On New Year's Eve "public spaces at Canary Wharf and the Thames river front were jammed with thousands of people whose reciprocal count-down could be heard from the top of the tower. Acres of newsprint coverage, with world-wide TV audience of multi-millions are testimony to the power of the event. Interestingly, the local reaction was overwhelmingly positive, in spite of the level of construction induced stress in the local population."

Art for the non-art venture

At what point and for what reason is the artist recruited by another sector? Is it in the hope that art will, by its place in a programme, help to make the venture more attractive? As recently as 1990 Sara Selwood pointed out that "the non-art input in public arts has conventionally come down to footing the bill."

'Public Art: Private Amenities', *Urban Design Quarterly*, 1990

The picture has shifted somewhat since then – in both directions. At Canary Wharf this country witnessed a major corporate investment in the arts quite different from sponsorship. For a year, Olympia and York funded, staffed and presented their own arts programme in London's Docklands. The arts formed part of an impressive bid to create one of the largest financial centres in Europe and inject cultural life into an otherwise under-populated environment. But since their bid failed, the arts programme's contribution to the developer's marketing strategy is unproven.

Under Helen Marriage's direction, events were selected to appeal to a non-art audience and to draw people into the spaces. Her £800,000 budget provided funds for lunchtime dance, music and visual arts events from companies who might otherwise have had little support for day-time activities. The programme received considerable publicity and drew thousands of people.

For corporate programmes in general, there are of course limitations. Forward planning is difficult and the financial successes and failures of the commercial company immediately shape the arts budget. There are inevitably restrictions on artistic experiment, given that the audience is not automatically prepared to take risks and looks to art for reassurance rather than challenge. Nevertheless Peter Fink, Anne Bean and Martyn Butler got the opportunity to collaborate on one of the UK's biggest budget, temporary public art events. The laser light show for Canary Wharf tower, commissioned to mark the arrival of 1992 was seen by thousands and relayed through national press coverage to millions more.

Community

It is not only the scale of art's marketing potential that attracts non-art organisations to bring artists into their lives. A parish council in a village in Cleveland with a total of 130 houses commissioned stone sculptures by Alain Ayers in 1988. Athough small in number, this was a closely knit community used to running events collaboratively. The village hall was used regularly for fundraising, celebration and social functions, so when Cleveland Arts invited them to discuss the possibility of establishing a

See also 'Hilton Parish New Milestones', *Local Arts UK*, November 1989 and 'Hilton New Milestones', Steve Chettle, *Local Council Review*, Spring 1990.

village sculpture project there was enthusiasm, and work on raising £3,500 began. Presented as part of Common Ground's New Milestones programme, the project was funded by Hilton Parish Council, Cleveland Arts and Northern Arts but the most impressive aspect of this project is the further support that was offered in kind which involved a commitment from a range of local people and business.

A local support group formed and the artist given free accommodation. A farmer gave labour and machines to move materials and scaffolding and stones were donated by local companies. Weekly

Circle by Richard Farringdon, one of the Skelton and Brotton New Milestones. Photo: Cleveland Arts

This 7' work is one of three metal sculptures made for the Cleveland Way.

meetings were a chance to air views and express any concerns. The artist's sensitivity to local anxieties and ability to incorporate all requirements into the final pieces has resulted in sculptures in which, three years after their completion, the village has great pride. Postmistress Dorothy Lewis explains how visitors are always shown the sites and given leaflets. She feels the benefits to the village far exceed the ownership of the art objects themselves. By witnessing the process of production and becoming totally involved in it, villagers had their eyes opened to the risks of art practice.

At first they couldn't understand why Ayers had produced no visible evidence of work in the first three months – now they recognise this was his research period to gather all the information he needed to channel into the making of appropriate sculptures for each site. Since completion of this project, villagers have displayed a new confidence in practice and presentation of the arts. They now contribute to Cleveland Visual Arts Festival with a display of their own work in the village hall.

Strengths & issues

Much of what has been explored here implies that there are real benefits to artists in working with others. But is there really strength in numbers or can the artist on his or her own outwit and upstage all collaborative potential?

Is there not something rather patronising in the way we develop forms of support for the arts which are always dependent on the artist working with someone else – be it gallery, local authority, commissions consultant, developer, TV producer or architect? Is there not inherent in this working method a belief that the artist cannot really manage alone, that the work has to be made 'relevant' to justify the level of funding – private or public – and as a result, that there is an eerie element of unspoken control over artistic experiment and risk?

Perhaps this is too gloomy a picture to paint. Surely there are enlightened collaborators who will and do make a real place for artists in their thinking. Sad to say, it is rarely the other way round. Artists are still on the outside when it comes to key planning, decision-making and financial control, rarely having the opportunity to determine for themselves the working processes, identify contexts and bring engineers, architects or administrators into their teams to work on projects instigated by them. There are few like Christo who command their own large-scale public projects right from the start, who establish the artistic parameters, raise the funds, negotiate with government, and employ the necessary skills to implement each work.

Whilst I am sympathetic to the notion of 'context' and 'relevance' when considering art for places, there is a danger that the art becomes a commodity on the production line of some organisation's output. It may become a crucial part of local authority strategy or a central plank of a developer's marketing policy, but if the artist has to jump through so many hoops to make the artwork relevant, sexy, popular, international, accessible, or whatever, where is the power of expression in that? How can artists be expected to challenge the visual status quo unless their projects can take root at an earlier stage in the debate?

Rick Faulkner feels: "Furthermore, public sector and corporate worlds in the UK militate against the individual in, for example, insurance and professional indemnity." There is inevitably more credibility given to a company than an individual, as clients nowadays are concerned with regulations and legal and financial restrictions. This coupled with the growth of compulsory competitive tendering leads to a requirement for artists to be evermore resourceful, businesslike and market-orientated, whilst at the same time retaining the vitality and vision which is the hallmark of any artist's contribution to the spirit of a place.

7 • Presentation

Eddie Chambers This chapter deals with some of the ideas and arguments relating to how artists can approach the task of presentation. That is, presentation of ideas and subsequently, presentation of completed work or work in progress. Because no matter how strong or attractive an idea might be or how confident an artist is that they can, with the right resources, successfully execute the idea, presentation may ultimately be the pivotal and decisive factor in a proposal's success or failure. Likewise, presentation of a finished commission requires considerable attention.

Before contemplating – and certainly before applying – for projects and commissions, artists must have adequate documentation of past work, whether or not their practice has previously involved making work outside galleries. Good visual documentation of an artist's previous work, primarily in 35mm slide form, is the starting point for all successfully negotiated projects.

Registers & indexes

AN Publications'
Factpack: Slide Indexes lists 36 indexes and registers describing who is eligible to join them, and who consults them.

Equipped with a good set of visual material, artists need to consider some of the ways in which they can manoeuvre themselves into positions where they are more likely to gain access to information about commissions and non-gallery based projects. One practical method is to lodge documentation of their work on all appropriate registers, indexes and slide libraries, particularly those consulted by curators, arts administrators and project facilitators.

Artists of African or Asian origin might consider depositing slides at the African and Asian Visual Artists Archive. Women artists might put slides in the files of the Women of Colour Slide Index or the Women Artists Slide Library – the former exists as an integral component of the latter. There are also other specialist agencies such as the London-based Public Art Development Trust and and Public Art Commissions Agency in Birmingham. These registers are regularly trawled by the

Making slides

Students should make maximum use of any plain white studio wall space within their college to regularly photograph their work. The point about the plain white background is critical, because much of the impact of paintings and sculpture is lost when the art work has to fight against a distracting background. Backdrops of cars, buildings, brickwork, and people should definitely be avoided, as should indoor backdrops of wallpaper, furniture, television sets and so on.

If plain white walls or clear uncluttered areas aren't available, students might collectively or individually approach a local gallery and 'borrow' wall space for a day or a few hours during less busy periods such as an exhibition change-over. It is worth working with other students to share costs of transportation, hire of lights, camera equipment and so on.

Beyond art school, artists should seek out suitable background walls and floors in their vicinity, and find out how they could make use of them. The need for a complementary background is critical. The gallery, agency or individual to whom an artist is making a proposal may be looking at several hundred slides at a time. In those circumstances the viewer grows rapidly impatient with slides of less than reasonable quality.

Avoid over-exposed or under-exposed slides, those that are out of focus and which feature anything at all other than the art work being documented. I've seen delightful slides of work featuring unintentional backdrops of erect ironing boards, switched on television sets, graffiti-covered brick walls and wonderful floral arrangements. Whilst these slides occasionally make fun photographs, they are a guaranteed turn-off when looked at in a professional slide-viewing session. If a slide looks good when it is placed on a light box it will look good when projected. The reverse is also true. Use daylight film for natural light and tungsten film for artificial lighting. To take your own slides, you don't need a sophisticated and expensive camera. All the documentation work I have done for the African and Asian Visual Artists Archive has been done using a Pentax K1000.

Original slides

Having arranged to photograph the work, maximise the opportunity by producing more than one set of slides. Either take multiple shots of each art work or the final set of slides can be duplicated at a photographic laboratory. The 'original' set of slides – if the latter method is chosen – should be clearly marked as such and kept safely. Under almost no circumstances should they be sent to accompany proposals. Recorded delivery or registered post are ultimately of little or no use if the slides get lost. A few years ago I delivered a set of 24 original slides to a major gallery in London. Having heard nothing from the gallery for several weeks, I telephoned, only to discover the slides had somehow been 'lost' or misplaced. Obliged to press the gallery for compensation, I received the then not insignificant sum of £200. But the money soon went, and I am still without those slides. Needless to say, the loss of those slides continues to have a marked and negative impact on the documentation of my work as an artist.

The message is clear. Duplicate your slides and treat them like the important and valuable commodity they are. No amount of money can compensate for the loss of original slides that cannot be retaken. When you make a series of work, document it immediately. Work that is lost, damaged, recycled or thrown away can never again be photographed. Make sure you fully exploit any exhibitions you have by taking 'installation' shots as well as slides of individual pieces.

Sending slides

Although glass-mounted slides keep careless greasy and acidic finger prints off the slide's delicate surface, even the most carefully packaged glass mounted slides often come to grief in the post. I've opened many padded envelopes to find a mess of splintered glass and scratched slides. Apart from being one of the worst possible introductions to an artist's work, broken glass-mounted slides are dangerous to human fingers and can seriously scratch valuable slides. Either pack glass-mounted slides snugly and adequately, or use clear stiff plastic slide holders known as slide journals.

The children's literature site at Parc Glynllifon developed by landscape architect Robert Camlin, environmental artist Ian Hunter and sculptor Denys Short with contributions from Sean Curley, Stuart Griffiths, Catrin Williams and Ann Catrin. Photo: Tamara Krikorian

Cywaith Cymru/ Artworks Wales, which puts art in the environment by commissions, exhibitions and residencies, has worked at Parc Glynllifon with Gwynedd County Council since 1984, developing writers in Gwynedd project which involves creation of new landscapes related to Welsh literature themes. Commissions for this and other sites are offered by open competition to artists in Wales.

agencies themselves or by groups and individuals seeking artists. Being represented on them may well give artists a decisive advantage over those who are not.

There is a more fundamental and important reason why agencies are important. By depositing slides and related biographical information with them, artists make a clear, decisive statement about the fact they exist, that as artists they are alive and practising. Artists can choose to affirm and state their existence and presence as artists and are, because of this, being written into contemporary art history. The question is this: as an artist, who knows of my existence? As an artist, how can I ensure a larger number of people know of my existence? Slide registers are usually a good first step.

An example of the positive use of slide libraries comes from Artworks Wales. When in collaboration with Marks and Spencer they set out to locate and identify a sculptor for a forthcoming public commission, they consulted no less than three different slide registers: the Welsh Arts Council Slide Registry, the Cardiff Bay Arts Trust index, and their own at Artworks Wales. Several sculptors were short-listed from these trawls and proposals commissioned. Put simply, those artists who were not represented on these any of these three indexes were not considered for the commission.

In my view, the regional arts associations have had a generally disastrous record of managing and operating slide registers. If you are considering depositing your slides with what are now regional arts board indexes, first get answers to several important questions. Firstly, does your RAB actually operate a slide register? If they do, who is responsible

AXIS – Visual Arts Information Service will establish a National Artists Register during 1993 and is working with others to devise cataloguing systems for contemporary work and a code of practice for the use of visual images.

for servicing and maintaining it? What access is offered to those seeking to look at slides? How is the slide register publicised to potential users?

As slides are valuable and important commodities, an artist can't afford the luxury of squandering their stock of slides. You have a right to ask the organisers of slide registers these and other pertinent questions. If you don't receive satisfactory answers, the best advice is to steer clear.

Review

If you deposit slides with registers, make sure you regularly update or complement them. An archaic and out-of-date collection of slides is of little or no use to viewers primarily interested in your recent output as an artist. Slides and CV should be updated annually, and critical information such as a change of address sent immediately. Artists should also ensure that slides and other documentation of their work are in no way being abused or misused in terms of copyright. If necessary, make a personal visit to registers that hold your slides. Seek reassurance and be reassured – or withdraw your slides.

Springboard

Your previous art practice should be viewed as a springboard for subsequent work which may be of a radically different nature. If you trained or are practising as a 'printmaker' or a 'painter', you are still able to execute a public commission as successfully as artists who have already had extensive experience of working in non-gallery environments. Your previous work may be just what makes you an attractive consideration. Documentation of your work indicates much more than just 'what you do'. It shows your working methodology, the ways you critically interpret or engage ideas, your aesthetics, your sensibilities and so on. These considerations are often used to assess an artist's work, rather than just looking at how good a 'painter' or a 'sculptor' he or she may be.

To summarise, those offering commissions, or able to facilitate your ideas, are more often than not concerned with how and with what consistency you have approached previous work, and are looking for clues to how you might approach a fresh commission or project.

Empowerment

There are important differences between the approach needed when artists apply for advertised commissions, and when artists seek to generate support and interest in their own propositions and ideas. A

What falls to the ground but can't be eaten, installation by Vong Phaophanit at Chisenhale Gallery, London 1991. Photo: African and Asian Visual Artists Archive

As part of a new waterfront development strategy, the London Borough of Greenwich sought two artists to develop permanently sited works in two areas of the Thames Barrier. Managed by Public Art Development Trust, the commissions were advertised nationally, the agency also using their own and the African and Asian Artists Archive slide register to contact potentially interested artists. From 170 applications, 17 artists were short-listed for interview. Commissions were awarded to Darrell Viner and Vong Phaophanit who both had work in the 1990 TSWA 'Four Cities' project. Chosen on the strength of previous installations rather than for his detailed proposal for the site, his outline proposal is to use architectural structures with volcanic ash and silk to create a piece which deals with barriers and boundaries and which will change with time because of the nature of the material, condensation, light and chemical reaction. The 30 x 4m work which will be presented behind a clear glass panel is due for completion in 1993.

suitable word to characterise this is 'empowerment'. One approach has a greater degree of control, autonomy and empowerment than the other.

If you apply for a widely advertised commission, without a doubt you'll be one of several hundred artists applying. Good slides, a clear and precise covering letter and a carefully and appropriately constructed CV should give you a decisive edge over lesser professional artists who also apply. Even so, most of the ideas and concerns informing the commission brief will be essentially of someone else's construction. As an artist, you will be responding to an imposed or predetermined brief. The best you can hope for is that someone will take a particular interest in your submission.

Even if you secure tentative or potential interest, you still need to go a considerable distance to convince those offering a commission you are a suitable candidate. This may involve interviews or submitting more detailed information. At all stages, the power to 'select' or 'develop' your proposal lies firmly with people other than you. You can hardly be said to be 'making your own way'.

If you choose to construct the terms of reference and creative parameters of a project wholly conceived and initiated by yourself, the process of personal empowerment becomes all too obvious. You may not ultimately succeed in executing your idea, but at all times you will have been in a more dignified and empowered position – one of unilaterally developing and seeking to execute your own ideas about art in public. Because you

Quarryman by Nick Moore.
Photo: the artist

The subject was the quarryman himself – the artist's 'ally'. He set out to create a life-size figure in stone of a working quarryman sited at the entrance to a thriving quarry at Combe Down in Bath. "The project was my own initiative. I approached quarryman John Hancock, who I have known for some time, and put the idea to him. He accepted on the spot, and a few drawings later the project was underway. He supplied the blocks of stone, one for the base and one of four tons for the figure and I worked the piece in situ under the gaze of quarrymen, customers and local residents."

can develop ideas more closely aligned to your personal position and situation, it can be argued that they stand a significant chance of realisation.

Environment

Firstly, you can determine the type of environment in which you would like to work. You might want to produce a temporary site-specific work or develop a more permanent piece of sculpture. Sensible research should make clear what localities and what environments you should consider.

A self-initiated project also allows you the vitally important possibility of developing a work that is consistent with your own political or social sensibilities and agendas. For instance, *The Quarryman* by Nick Moore is a piece of sculpture the artist feels is his personal "tribute to the generations of unsung heroes who laboured day in day out, in dust and danger, to extract stone which went into the celebrated buildings we can still appreciate today. It also cemented a long friendship with the quarrying environment and allowed me to give something back to this natural source of wealth that can only be used once."

Partners

Through sensible research, you should be able to ascertain the companies, land owners, local authority departments, tenants and so on who need to be approached. If you are making unsolicited approaches to these people, using skill, tact, and persuasion, you may be able to develop your idea and enter into a fruitful dialogue with them.

This may involve pin-pointing the appropriate individual within a company, building, council department or whatever. Here, the idea of finding and nurturing prospective and sympathetic 'allies' becomes of central importance. Such individuals may need to be strategically located. After all, the future of a proposal may rest with an individual or a group of individuals saying "yes, why not... let's give this artist a chance."

Fundraising

Unilaterally developing a proposal may involve raising funds or sponsorship. It may be that, having made sufficient progress in locating the site and the potential partners, an artist chooses to raise the money needed by taking temporary employment. Realistically, sources of public money are severely limited, so sponsorship may need to be found. However, consider any regional arts board award schemes, local community or arts budgets, government community development funds and so on. There is always the option of direct requests for financial assistance to relevant individuals and companies. Because of the unique and specific nature of Nick Moore's project, the quarryman helped to a considerable degree by supplying the stone.

Guidelines governing raising sponsorship and the development of ideas for site-specific non-gallery based work hardly differ between artists responding to a brief and artists unilaterally developing a brief, although there is a fundamental difference of power and empowerment between the two approaches.

It is my view that a focused, agile and creative artist can make much headway with developing unsolicited proposals, simply because he or she at all times maintains a critical degree of control. After all, an artist has much less to 'lose' if his or her unilaterally developed ideas ultimately bear little or no fruit.

Responses to a brief

It is important now to look at how artists can most effectively respond to a brief speculatively presented to them. In most likely cases – apart from those adventurous artists who would rather be assertively pro-active – this will be a commission for which they are applying.

Artists need to be aware they have the ability to affect and alter the parameters and nature of any given brief, providing they sensitively, tactfully and confidently word and structure their applications and use the same skills and approaches at the interview stage.

This will involve tactfully offering ideas and suggestions as to how they – the artist – would, if given the opportunity, seek to improve or otherwise develop the brief. Any brief may have its flaws, but it is essential artists point these out and suggest improvements in a tactful and diplomatic way.

Even a well-defined brief is only a starting point. Artists who successfully negotiate commissions may, if they rely too heavily and uncritically on what has already been drawn up, find themselves with no alternative but to take responsibility for any flaws or problems that may develop within the commission.

Artists shouldn't be reluctant to demonstrate that a brief has been fully understood, with an appropriate degree of critical intelligence. From a technical point of view, there could be serious technical flaws

Permindar Kaur's *Copper Speakers*, Glasgow, May 1992. **Photo:** the artist

This artist, whose slides are in the African and Asian Artists Archive, was invited to make a proposal for the BBC Billboard Art Project. "Two sculptural billboards face each other over a busy pedestrian area, on one three copper megaphone/flower forms, underneath a rubber emblem of a lotus flower, a wheel and the initials PK in Punjabi. Opposite is one larger megaphone/flower surrounded by a green tile pattern of an 8-sided star. The 'speakers' physically pushing through revealing the sky behind are silently communicating with each other above traffic and pedestrians. Enigmatic and intriguing, a suggestion as to whom and what the speakers are saying is implied by rubber emblems and tile pattern. Billboards, usually seen with bold designs, have been replaced by a more subtle, meditative and abstract message."

See also 'Applications & Proposals'.

which are not obvious to those who are not artists. When speculatively applying for a commission, artists shouldn't be afraid to point them out, and tactfully make suggestions to overcome or avoid them.

When responding to a brief:

- have a clear and well written/constructed CV
- use a good quality set of well-selected slides
- send carefully selected supplementary material
- give a clear indication the brief has been properly read and understood.

Interviews

Having made it to the short-listing stage, an artist may be called to an interview, or required to make a formal or informal 'presentation'. If those offering the commission are committed to equal opportunities, the interview stage should give you a fair chance to convince interviewers that your proposals are worth developing.

Although interviews tend to follow a standard formula and advice on interview procedures and tactics is generally available, these comments may be of some to artists when dealing with formal interviews.

Make sure you fully understand the terms and nature of the brief. If possible, undertake some 'reconnaissance' or familiarisation visits to the proposed site. It shouldn't be too difficult to anticipate the types of questions that may be asked at an interview. Artists should not be overly

440 Lights, an installation based on lines of lights and reflections exploring 2-D perspective in a 3-D context by John Forster and Steve Bull **for Eastgate Shopping Centre, Gloucester, December 1991. Photo:** the artists

"In terms of presenting our work, if we are well-prepared, we feel we are halfway there. We have packs prepared on all our projects, these include slides, photographs, press releases, posters and sometimes the proposals themselves. We are now developing special folders to hold everything in a logical way."

hesitant to seek advice from other 'successful' artists, or artists who have previously successfully negotiated commissions.

Mock interviews may also be useful, particularly if an artist has had little or no experience of formal interviews. An artist, who prefers to remain anonymous, went to eight interviews and was rejected each time until a sympathetic interviewer told him that to sweat visibly and wring his hands did not inspire confidence. After two hours of mock interviews he went on to win his first major residency.

Know your strengths and weaknesses in relation to the proposed commission. If there are other artists or technicians with whom you would like to collaborate on specific aspects of the commission, don't be afraid to say so. It may be that additional funds can be secured for this. The interviewers will want a response to "why do you want to do this commission?" "What skills or experience can you offer the project?" "How will you undertake and successfully complete the commission?" If the commission marks a dramatic shift away from your previous practice, you are likely to be asked to explain the reasons behind this move.

Interviewees should be pleasant and enthusiastic, but not to a suffocating or irritating degree. Make as much generalised eye contact as possible with the interviewers. Looking at the floor for the duration of the interview will hardly impress. If you need to be reassured or reminded of key points in your proposal, take a copy to refer to. Take time before answering complicated or difficult questions, but a few seconds should never be allowed to become awkward and extended silences. If you feel very nervous or make a mistake, feel free to take a deep breath, or ask for a glass of water.

Metropolis by Robert Koenig.
Photo: the artist

A chance visit by *The Times* newspaper's arts journalist to see the making of this piece in Milton Keynes brought with it a wonderful assortment of press and media goodies. As well as a photo-news item in the national paper, Koenig explains the 'mobilisation' effect: "This coverage in turn mobilised a free-lance news gathering crew filming for Sky TV and other local television news programmes." The unveiling of the sculpture brought both Anglia and Central TV who produced news items on the same day. Local newspapers also covered it. This invaluable media coverage, much of which was generated by commissioners Milton Keynes Development Corporation, was supplemented by articles in two specialist woodworker magazines. These came about because a local freelance photographer – with the sculptor's permission – supplied photographs.

Two-way process

Artists being interviewed should remember that interviews are essentially a two-way process. The interview is your opportunity to find out more about the commission, and to be assured that you know exactly what it involves. Questions about expenses, fees, budgets, timetables and so on will assure interviewers you have understood and are serious about the project. The vitally important thing is to make sure you have made all your points clearly, and have clarified any queries you had. On no circumstances go horrendously over your time allocation. It's selfish, it pisses people off and is unfair on just about everybody involved, particularly those being interviewed after you.

Visual presentation

If you have the opportunity to make a visual presentation, it's worth doing so. Anticipate what the interview panel are likely to want to know, check

Making a presentation work

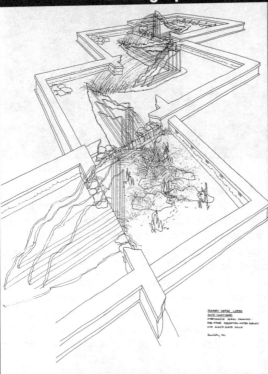

QUARRY HOUSE LEEDS
RIVER COURTYARD
INVESTIGATIVE AERIAL DRAWING :
3RD PHASE SEQUENTIAL WATER DISPLAY
WITH SLICED SLATE HILLS

Investigative aerial drawing by Susan Tebby for the 3rd phase of a sequential water display with sliced slate hills at Quarry House Leeds, the new headquarters for the Departments of Health and Social Security.

To be completed in 1993, Susan Tebby's commission comprises an integrated landscape work in which water is the unifying theme. Two 36 x 42m courtyards incorporate designed and sculptural elements to provide a secluded, tranquil environment for up to 3000 people working there. As a focus, pools with sequential water displays are programmed to change appearance during the day, with the maximum effect between 12 noon and 2pm when people may wish to sit outside.

Interest in her work from potential commissioners encouraged her to produce a video describing thought processes behind and documentation of a painted constructive environment *Layered Lattices*, commissioned by Hammersmith Hospital through Public Art Development Trust and completed in 1989. Video and accompanying handbook were shown at the World Trade Fair Rotterdam in 1990 and are used to promote her work generally. "Once, when unable to attend a presentation to bid for a commission, I sent a voice tape to accompany my portfolio and subsequently got the work.

"I have a gadget for transferring slides and negatives of work to video, particularly useful for sending work to Europe. I use a thermo binding machine and a comb binder to make proposals into booklets.

"The fax machine has been my best buy. I can send photographs and A1 drawings cut into A4 width strips to clients, architects or sub-contractors, so that their comments can be added and faxed back within a short time. It saves days of travel, post and time."

Head for the Hills, mosaic mural at Manchester Royal Infirmary's Department of Psychiatry made in 1989 by artists working with patients in the START community arts project. **Photo:** Jack Sutton

Winner of the visual arts category in a BBC competition for community initiatives, this was featured in the *British Medical Journal* and arts and regional press. As well as working in Manchester hospitals, START provides opportunities for members and artists to undertake paid environmental art commissions in a variety of community settings.

how many minutes you will get and stick to the time limit. Presentations give an artist the opportunity to control and direct that part of the interview. Emphasise and illustrate your strengths, and refer to any previous projects that may not have been entirely successful in a tactful and sensible way.

There are relative yet distinct shifts in power and influence when artists successfully move from applying for a commission to securing one for themselves. Whilst skill, tact, and diplomacy are still much needed at this stage, artists are in a more favourable position with regard to adapting, improving or re-defining the brief.

Launch

Having successfully executed a commission, the artist should turn their attention to the 'launching' end of the process. This is as important stage as any other, and refers directly to the points raised earlier in the chapter. The launching or unveiling of a commission should be exploited to the maximum by the artist. If a piece is temporary, exhaustive photographic documentation should be done, particular if the piece is likely to be damaged by 'vandalism' or the elements. 'In progress' documentation should obviously have been done along the way. If a piece is permanent, it needs to be documented in a 'pristine' state to use for launch publicity and to promote yourself later to future commissioners.

A Norwich Union advertising campaign subverted by AVI.
Photo: AVI

"AVI is a group of textual gangsters with access to DTP technology and a background in semiotics. Work is language based: immediate, hard-hitting and very temporary. [One example] was an adaption of a Hennes poster at Oxford Circus that had the line 'It will suit your bank manager' next to a girl dressed in a £9.99 skirt and £3.99 top. This was transformed in broad daylight by the addition 'Don't pay the poll tax' in matching lettering. It didn't last long, probably about six hours. But that was long enough for it to feature in *Time Out, The Standard, Socialist Worker* as well as *Campaign*, the advertising trade magazine."
(Naomi Salaman)

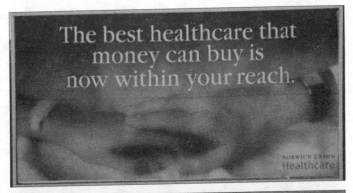

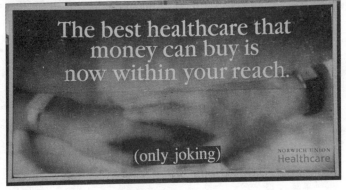

Strategy

When drawing up a strategy for a launch, consider the following questions:

- What will be the best and most effective publicity strategy?
- How can artists effectively collaborate with agencies and others assigned to launching and promoting the finished commission?
- Where can artists get advice on how to secure good press and media coverage?

Don't underestimate the importance of writing concise and appealing press releases and of having a stock of good press and publicity photographs for press and media use.

There are occasions when press coverage has a 'snowballing' effect, when an initial press story encourages others to follow it up. Journalists often scan magazines and newspapers for hints of stories or items that they can pursue or develop. A small piece in a local newspaper may lead to more sizable press coverage, and a decent sized piece in a national newspaper can set all sorts of press and media wheels in motion.

By the time you come to consider the most suitable way of launching or unveiling a piece of work, all people connected with its making should be able to assist with the launch in a positive way. In the case of the *Metropolis* sculpture, a two-hour 'unveiling' ceremony which included poetry and improvised jazz was organised by the rangers in whose park the carved column was sited.

8 • Developing the artwork

Lee Corner As popularity for contemporary visual art placed outside the gallery has grown, the role and function of the artist/maker has diversified.

From one extreme to the other, the artist has been encouraged to site work in places independent of the nature of the place or the views of those who have to live with it, or to engage on long-term familiarisation projects, sometimes taking up residence in a location to ensure the relevance of the finished artwork to both site and community.

Many artists working outside the gallery express their desire to be used as a consultant as well as a producer, feeling the work and partnerships involved give them an opportunity to make an impact on wider aspects of the world and larger audiences than galleries allow. They see the chance to make a real contribution to the inclusion of art in people's everyday lives as well as a comparatively rare opportunity to be paid for their expertise and experience as well as their product!

Undoubtedly much could be achieved simply by locating one of their artworks in a public site. But for most, the real chance to have an impact seems to come from the potential offered by engaging more directly with a whole raft of 'partners' – commissioners, designers, engineers, fellow artists, passive and active users.

The majority of artists and 'commissioners' agree the quality of the dialogue between them is as much a factor in achieving a quality end-product as practical factors such as site, material and technical skill.

First encounters

The ideal relationship is one of mutual respect and recognition: by the artist for the commissioner's intention and motivation; by the commissioner for the artist's interpretation and skill. This 'ideal' will be affected positively or negatively by the earliest stages of the encounter.

For example, if the commissioner has produced a clear brief, has done some homework and can articulate the reasons and intentions for the inclusion of art, artists contemplating making a bid might reasonably be expected to decide whether they are interested in that job. If they can't relate to the information provided, it may not be worth pursuing.

When Jane Kelly and David Patten received the *Invitation Document for the Appointment of a Lead Artist* from Sheffield City Polytechnic for its £80 million development plan Campus 21, they received a clear, confident and well articulated summary of the aims and objectives for the involvement of artworks and artists in the development.

See also 'Applications & proposals'

In return, Kelly and Patten responded with a 'package' of information comprising slides, studies and proposals for previous work and catalogues, all well-produced and showing the breadth of their skills and experience. They describe this package as "a generous investment" not least because it represented some £60 worth of material!

Moreover, the initial meeting for short-listed candidates took the form of a presentation by the commissioners based on their own research into art in public in Britain and the USA, presentations by other members of the development team – architects, developers, etc – and a comprehensive site visit.

Jane and David state unequivocally: "We were able to produce a good response to the brief because it was clear and comprehensive without being overly directive. They had done their research thoroughly and in asking us to take them seriously, they were indicating that they would take us seriously."

Their subsequent appointment as lead artists was to some extent the result of this initial establishment of mutual respect and recognition. But if a well-prepared brief and well-prepared response were the only factors in achieving this, the answer to the commissioner/artist relationship would be easy. Unfortunately (or fortunately?) other factors come into play, not least of which are the inexpressible issues of personal philosophy, ideology, taste or just plain inter-personal chemistry!

In this example the commissioner's brief triggered a recognition or response in the artists. Their return submission then triggered a recognition in the commissioner. There was some level of mutual understanding beyond the written words, though contained within the language and ideas both were using.

Checklist

- If you can't relate to a brief think carefully about going further – the first trigger may have failed.
- If you do/can relate to it, see your response as an investment and recognise that investments can fail as well as produce dividends.

Making an application

Jane Kelly **and** David Patten **putting up an exhibition to support their proposal. Photo:** Chris Lawton

In April 1992, Jane Kelly and David Patten were appointed Lead Artists for the Campus 21 development programme at Sheffield City Polytechnic now Sheffield Hallam University.

For this multi-million scheme, they will work as part of a design team, their focus being the development of a concept and philosophy for art in public, a schematic plan and methodology, identification of sites, routes and opportunities, materials and themes and a framework for the involvement of other design teams. The overall theme will be materials, with stone, steel and water symbolising the city's industrial history.

The initial phase, to be completed by summer 1993, is to revitalise the Pond Street area by incorporating into the polytechnic site a public thoroughfare, so that it acts as a link between a proposed media centre and the city's Lyceum and Crucible Theatre, helping to create a 'cultural quarter'. By the end of 1995, two further phases will be complete. By appointing artists in the planning stages, Peter Downey (principal assistant in the polytechnic's resource planning department) says: "Art will not be an add-on extra, but an essential part of the design."

In their initial application and proposal Kelly and Patten – who have worked collaboratively in the past – describe what it would be like to walk to the Pond Street site once the development is finished. "We leave the station, and use the pedestrian crossing to cross busy Sheaf Street to reach the corner of the Student Union Building. Previously, the dark angled façades were blank, but now their ugly awkwardness has been transformed and integrated into a remarkable letter-form relief proudly announcing location and place. The large scale and striking colour/material of the design link it visually to the new 'A' block. The gates between the buildings have been pushed back, and what was once a rather poky and cluttered pavement 'gateway' is now the start of a beautifully landscaped linear park which fronts the polytechnic as far as Harmer Lane. We turn right... the route to the Sheaf Street entrance opens before us and a line of mature trees marks the way....

"The park provides sheltered enclosures and impressive vistas, its spiral configuration mirroring the movement of the sun, and the seating an opportunity to meet or rest.

"It feels open, welcome and safe...planting is lush and a recent shower of rain enhances the aroma of blossom and bark. Bicycle rests and the strong simple lines of lighting, litter bins and bollards sit comfortably among carefully considered hard and soft landscaping.... In the entrance, we mount stone steps and brass inlay inscriptions in the risers glow in the morning sun.... Entering the glazed concourse, the decorative floor continues and is animated by the light coming through the translucent, richly coloured roof. Everything invites entrance, not only to reach our specific destination, but for the enrichment of experience it promises."

- Think of their brief and your response as the beginnings of a dialogue. Respond to the triggers they produce and offer your own for them to respond to. Avoid being overly prescriptive at this stage and don't try to pre-empt the continuing dialogue.
- Begin to establish 'The Relationship of Mutual Respect'! Do some homework on commissioner or client. Be confident without being arrogant.
- Wear smart clothes – though some say not too smart!
- Find ways of showing that as an artist you are also a practical person. Be realistic, show attention to detail.

Consultant/artist

The notion of 'consultant' elicits mixed feelings. Consultants are frequently seen as insatiable amoebae, recreating themselves by ingesting vast quantities of cash – which would otherwise be available for 'the practice'.

Alternatively the consultant is interpreter of the client's stated and unstated desires, the animator making realities of dreams.

To act as the latter, artists must be able to listen and to hear what the client wants. They must also be able to facilitate those dreams and desires by channelling them into achievable tasks. A secure sense-of-self and a realistic knowledge of personal strengths and abilities are crucial if an artist/consultant is to convey this confidence and win the client's trust.

In an article on a Paris symposium on public art, Roland Miller describes the cultural differences which make the consultant/artist a reality in France and, as yet, often a dream in Britain. "A proposition from French speakers was that artists could commission architects for new developments... that artists can contribute solutions to planning problems that are not aesthetic, but social, educational or demographic. The artist has a legitimate role in what the French call 'urbanisme' and we call 'town planning'."

'Art · public, rencontres internationales autour de la creation dans la ville et l'environnement', held at the Musée d'Art Moderne de la Ville de Paris, October 1990

Some notable examples exist in Britain and perhaps the trend is growing. John Maine was appointed to the Lewisham 2000 design and build team in 1989 not, as might have been the case in earlier years, to contribute the odd bit of sculpture to the complete remodelling of the town's centre, but to join the 15-strong team of planners and engineers as a catalyst for creative problem-solving. Three and a half years later, his role has evolved into membership of the commissioning committee which identifies artists for autonomous art works within the new design.

Artist/consultant

Ceiling and floor pieces at Tabor High School. Photo: David Bartram, Essex County Council

Brennand Wood's **14' x 14' x 9' ceiling piece – an exploration of calligraphic forms on the theme of movement and flight – is made of painted and dyed rope, bound metal, fabric and wire, constructed in 80 suspended units. The 13' diameter floor, designed by him and made collaboratively with furniture maker** Nick Pryke**, is inlaid with painted wood, oak and maple and set into resin, its design inspired by Andreas Cellanius' 1660 celestial atlas *Harmonia Macrocosmica.*

When Essex County Council started planning the building of Tabor High School in Braintree, Arts Development Officer David Dougan suggested the architects should include an artist in the design team. With the help of Public Art Development Trust, Michael Brennand Wood was chosen as consultant.

Starting in September 1989, he was first involved in the planning stages, later identifying commission opportunities, suggesting artists and makers and helping to manage the project, which was completed in October 1992. The project won the first 'Art for Architecture' award given by the Royal Society for the encouragement of Arts, Manufactures and Commerce (RSA).

Excited by the project's potential, he didn't assume that a building is automatically 'enhanced' by art, realising that this depends very much on the architecture and architects' attitudes.

He worked closely with project architect Ian Fraser throughout the design stage. As this evolved, he generated proposals which the team of six artists and makers could develop in the context of the building's aesthetic and functional requirements, the result being that art works look as if they were designed specifically for the building.

Choice of artists was influenced by their creative and technical abilities and their experience of working to commission. He also looked for those who wanted to extend their skills in new directions and to work with new materials or approaches.

The creative catalyst model of consultancy also informed Michael Brennand Wood's invitation to the design team of Essex County Council's new Tabor High School development. When Property Services embarked on the design of the new school, it was agreed art should be integrated into the architectural process from the outset. Brennand Wood was stimulated by working with with the architect, the creative relationship sparking off ideas and changing his work. "A successful commission is one in which dialogue with the architects starts as early as possible and in which both are stimulated to come up with solutions which are surprising to both." Equally, Fraser has enjoyed working with him, stimulated by his choice of materials and use of interior spaces.

Brennand Wood's attention to detail – to lighting, landscaping, use of interior spaces – as well as his input to the achieving of "a more cohesive, visually exciting building", was particularly welcomed.

Attention to detail is an interesting factor in the design process and not one usually attributed to stereotypical artists with their unrealistic and grandiose notions. Even in the early stages Kelly and Patten, working as lead artists in Sheffield, have been able to point out practical problems which might result from an etched plate glass screen in the new polytechnic's central atrium. Kelly was particularly interested to know whether the designers had taken into account the cleaning factor – who would clean this screen, how much time would it take, how would its farthest reaches be accessed. She attributes this awareness not just to being an artist with "an attention to detail" but to being the only woman on the team and thus in sympathy with the inevitable army of women cleaners for the building!

Artist/consultant

In each of these examples, Maine, Brennand Wood and Kelly/Patten have been involved in a process of creating an environment sympathetic to receiving artworks. Part of their work has been to pave the way for other artists whose remit will be to produce artworks.

The majority of artists working outside the gallery in Britain today fall into this category. They might work directly with the commissioner, on their own initiative, within a public art agency's stable, or through a consultant/artist as described above.

They might still be used as consultants but the extent will depend on who they are working with and how the project is organised. It is within this broad field that the artist is most vulnerable. Too many examples exist of artists being paid less for their time and expertise than other

Developing a project

Those Environmental Artists,
Shirt at **Upper Campfield Market, 1991. Photo:** TEA

Living Space Manchester, the third of a series of investigations into the multiple role of the house as a symbol and a place, was devised and created in 1991 by Those Environmental Artists (Val Murray, Jon Biddulph, Lynn Pilling and Peter Hatton) for Manchester's Upper Campfield Market, a former second-hand clothes market.

Living Spaces were also created at Stoke Museum and Art Gallery where they installed a life-sized scaffold house clad in biscuit ware, and in Liverpool as part of the 'New Art North West' exhibition when different versions of armchair, lamp, table and TV were installed in a burned-out warehouse, empty shop, billboard site and park.

Background

After unsuccessful negotiations in the summer of 1990 with the Museum of Labour History, TEA proposed *Living Spaces* for the September 1991 Manchester Festival. An enthusiastic Director helped them to raise from Central Manchester Development Corporation and North West Arts the £6000 budget needed to realise the installation – three giant 'garments' constructed from real clothes, suspended from the roof structure, secured at the bottom and opened out to form sheltered spaces illuminated by light bulbs. Concerned about the load-bearing capacity of the market's cast iron roof, city architects and engineers insisted on installation of an internal support structure adding £300 to the budget. The council also demanded an unexpected £1000 licence fee to use the space. To gain permission from the environmental health officer required fire-proofing the garments, installing fire extinguishers, no smoking regulations and agreement that food wouldn't be prepared on site.

Installation

Installation took the form of a four-week TEA residency, the first few days used to co-ordinate incoming scaffolders, sewing machines, fire extinguishers and other services. The clothing, bought in bulk from an Oxfam Wastesaver Centre, had already been collected, the quantity needed carefully calculated according to the dimensions of building and 'garments'. Using two industrial sewing machines, rails of fire-proofed garments were assembled in to sections, pinned to giant 'patterns' and sewed into three enormous garments – dress, trousers

Installing *Living Space* – a 25' high scaffold framework clad in biscuit ware – at Stoke City Museum and Art Gallery in 1991. Photo: City Museum and Art Gallery

and shirt – for display on roof-based hangers. It took three people to lift, fold and machine the final seams, the shirt completed at the end of the first week. For an evening celebratory event, music was commissioned from Dan Morrison based on the sounds of sewing machines, clothes being washed, scissors cutting and other related sounds. Continuous tapes were sited inside each garment and in a fourth piece made from a festoon of light bulbs.

Documentation

The project's progress was shown on Granada TV's 'Celebration', the installation itself in *The Guardian*, *City Life* and the *Manchester Evening News*.

TEA

"We make temporary structures and events in public places and are concerned with the commonplace to provide a common visual language. Our aim is to shift perceptions, thus art making is a form of research and observation which highlights what there is as well as what is missing, passes comment, makes new connections as well as transforming. We explore the interactions of place, process and materials."

The artists work individually and collectively, organising on average two TEA projects a year. For 1992/94, they are working with Impossible Theatre on 'Other People's Shoes', a project funded through the Arts Council's 'New Collaborations' scheme.

professionals, not being able to effect change within the initial brief, and not having their views respected.

The contributing factors to this vulnerability are worth noting. If an artist is working directly for a commissioner, at least there is the chance of direct dialogue. However, especially if working alone, the potential for being swamped by expectations, overruled by authority or used as a pawn in someone else's political chess game is often present.

An artist's own initiative – identifying a site, knowing what to put there, working with a community – offers an apparent freedom. But spinning plates is an exhausting and sometimes thankless task, and although funding can be raised for a project it is rarely enough to cover the fundraising effort itself, the negotiating, the consultation and the sleepless nights.

Working with an agency or similar body also has advantages and disadvantages. Ideally, an agency acts as a buffer against fundraising problems, multiple agendas and intransigent commissioners. However, it is also a buffer to direct dialogue, which for many artists is an adrenalin source for new ideas and creative solutions.

In this latter area, the artist/consultant (and indeed the consultant/artist) has much to offer and gain. They can offer the commissioner a kind of permission to do something above the ordinary and expected and can facilitate a raising of expectations. For this to happen the crucial relationship of respect has to be in place.

Kelly and Patten were consulted on the treatment of the hoardings which will surround the site once building on the new Sheffield Polytechnic starts. The idea proposed to them was to use school children, free emulsion paint and a professional artist guiding-hand. They began to explore the function of hoardings and people's reaction to them: at best, frustration because they can't see what's going on, at worst alienation from whatever's being built because even passively, they can't be part of its creation. The result was a total reconsideration of how best to create the safety and security barrier between public and building site. Perspex, metal lattice work, projected images will all need to be considered in relation to cost, but the collective imagination can now pursue new ways of dealing with an old problem.

'Creating a Relationship of Mutual Respect' isn't a title that appears on most training agencies' lists! Understanding that it is a prerequisite to the achievement of a mutually acceptable goal is the first hurdle, and 'chemistry' is certainly a factor.

Yet the artist can take a pro-active role in achieving such a relationship. Showing respect for commissioner and brief is a starting point. Researching background information, listening to what is being

Paul Stone, *Have Your Cake and Eat It*, a 145 x 101cm cibachrome image permanently sited at West London Hospital in 1991

When Paul Stone was commissioned to produce work for Riverside Studios' 'Art and About' project at West London Hospital's ante-natal clinic, staff had already had a chance to see his work and contribute their comments: "I was told early on that some of my work wouldn't be suitable due to it being potentially 'upsetting' or even 'offensive' to the space's users, a viewpoint I could appreciate and see as a challenge and not a constraint." In appreciating the staff's understanding of their clients and patients, Stone was also respecting their professional assessment. His willingness to re-direct his work was called upon in the latter stages of the project when staff explained that his image of a baby feeding from a bottle countered their own encouragement to mothers to breastfeed.

said, asking relevant questions, and beginning the dialogue are ways of signalling this.

Self-confidence is a significant factor. As Jane Kelly puts it: "In the early stages everything we do says – 'We are artists; we articulate; we collaborate; we consult; we respond visually'."

Checklist

- Be confident about your skills, experience, expertise and knowledge. You are a fellow professional.
- Suggest you might be part of an overall team. Show willingness to attend planning meetings and discussions. By being in on conversations you have the chance to put in your views and ideas, and surprises are less likely to be foisted on you.
- Do not belittle other people's ideas or views. If they need challenging, do so diplomatically.

Siting a commission

Nancy Willis, artist in residence at the Special Care Baby Unit at Hammersmith Hospital from September 1990 to March 1992 in a project managed by Public Art Development Trust, worked in a studio provided by the hospital to make a work for siting in the hospital.

Beginning by making drawings of sick and premature babies, she developed them into colour drawings in the studio. "The sheets on which the babies lay began to look like the slopes of a landscape. In one, I turned the nasal feeding tube into a green stem, sprouting leaves and painted the baby amongst autumn leaves to make her new life the more fragile and precious. I set the painting in a shallow fruit box made rich by sanding and painting with layers of shellac and traces of gold leaf.

"To counter clinical whites and hard surfaces, I put red velvet around the painting in the box, suggesting mysterious moss or the remains of a soft womb.

Nancy Willis' **commissioned work in progress. Photo:** Gina Glover

"I drew breast-feeding mothers, one I chose to put with the baby and leaf landscape. With fragility and preciousness in mind, I made a print on fine blue tissue painted with gold of the baby being breast-fed. A shellacked fruit box contained this image.

"The two boxed images together made an icon-like construction. I added half a wooden cheese box to make a curved arch at the top. In this I put a relief model of a baby wrapped by his mother's hand. To connect the three parts, I attached a plastic vine to the boxes, completing the metaphor begun by transforming the feeding tube.

"When the work was well advanced, I presented it to the hospital's art committee. Little was said at the time, but I was told later they thought it should not go up in a public part of the hospital. They thought it too morbid and upsetting, dwelling on life's fragility.

"It took some weeks to resolve this difficulty. Fortunately, I had access to a display case where I could show my work and get feedback more generally. Once the work was well displayed, it looked good. I left a comments book which gained enthusiastic responses.

"I then had the chance to look at the work afresh with some of the committee who began to feel more positive about it. Finally, with the supportive intervention of the manager of the Neo-Natal Unit, it was agreed the work would be sited in the waiting area of the new Special Care Baby Unit in Spring 1993."

- Keep asking questions. Don't pretend to understand if you haven't. Help people to make themselves clear: what people mean is not always what they say first time round.

Negotiation

Artists working in public appear to be almost unanimous in rejecting the notion of 'compromise', preferring softer terms such as 'challenge' or 'problem-solving'. Behind this reaction lies something of the essence of why artists work to commission.

Compromise smacks of a negative response to the practical forces which necessitate change from an original idea or concept. If the negative connotation is taken away, what is left is a potentially exciting and creative process of evolution and review. Add the element of collaboration or collective response – creative problem solving – and the attraction of working in this field begins to emerge.

Val Murray summarises the advantages as "real problem solving; using more of my skills than just making sculpture – I enjoy organising and negotiating! Satisfaction comes from a feeling that you have not compromised but have responded imaginatively and with insight to the context and provoked some kind of response – not necessarily applause!"

Whether the negotiation is taking place at the outset of a commission or during the process, the style in which it is conducted is important. In the ideal world of mutual respect, recognition and trust, such issues might not occur, but for those still working to achieve the ideal, it is worth considering the thin line between conviction and arrogance!

Accusations of arrogance might be well founded but equally often it is the word used by someone in a position of authority to describe someone who appears to be challenging that authority. Back in the stereotypical world of the artist starving in the garret, some commissioners might find it extraordinary and unnerving to meet articulate, self-confident artists, familiar with expressing their views.

Conviction, on the other hand, is generally applauded. Negotiating successfully is thus a matter of style. Neither the shrinking violet nor the head-butting bully elicit much respect. Doug Cocker believes that the approach affects the art. "The trick is to seek, and with luck, find or create the situation in which there is freedom. An awful lot of contemporary public art fails to work because of individual arrogance. Nearly all the beautiful places or exciting places that have been left to us are so simply because of compromise or collaboration."

The unveiling of Sue Jane Taylor's *Piper Alpha Memorial* sited in the North Sea Rose Garden, Hazel Head Park, Aberdeen in 1991. Photo: Murdo MacLeod

The artist faced particular challenges on this commission. "Having worked on the subject of the oil worker and the oil industry's presence in Scotland for six years, being chosen and commissioned to work on the memorial was a natural progression in my work. Because I had been on the platform and drawn some of the men later killed in the disaster, I felt very much involved. The Piper Alpha Memorial Committee had strong views about the memorial: the majority of its members were bereaved families. I had to tread carefully. Through lengthy discussions, we came to an agreement where both parties were happy with the maquette. Confidence and a good working relationship were brought about by showing the committee every stage of the sculpture's development.... The memorial became a homage for 167 families and especially for the 33 families whose loved ones' bodies were never recovered. Fresh flowers are constantly lain by it. I involved families by having an open studio for them to visit me during the sculpture's making. A survivor volunteered to become one of the life models."

Checklist

- Be clear in your own mind where your 'bottom line' is. This is vital in maintaining integrity and self-respect.
- Recognise negotiation as a potentially creative process rather than one of being beaten down.
- Have passion and the courage of your convictions but don't let them become blocks to hearing others' opinions.

Consultation

If negotiation is about arriving at mutually acceptable solutions, consultation is about identifying what might need to be solved. Throughout a collaborative process involving other professionals – architects, planners,

The *Norse Longship* created for an animated trail, developed through a Company of Imagination residency and training course commissioned by the Countryside Commission of Scotland in 1991. Photo: Company of Imagination

This multi-arts company makes links between arts and the environment and works with rural communities to explore and celebrate the spirit of a place. Projects include animated trails, outdoor promenade performances or pageants, semi-permanent sculptures using found material or permanent plaques, reliefs or sculptures. The local community or visitors to a site are involved in the process of creation and presentation. Focus, duration, scope and nature of each project are jointly agreed with client or commissioner. A team of between four and six artists/ tutors – who usually have a range of making and performing skills – is drawn from a freelance pool of people with whom the company has worked before. A five-day project using five artists would cost a client around £3500.

environmentalists, engineers and so on – the processes of consultation and negotiation will be inseparable.

However, there comes a point in most projects – preferably sooner rather than later – when those who are going to have to interact with the overall design or individual artwork, passively or actively, need to be consulted.

This is often the most difficult and rewarding interface and many artists agree with Val Murray that access to a wider audience is why they engage in such work. "Exposure to a wider audience, feedback, interaction. These become important ingredients to the way the work develops."

The issue of consultation is not just about creating a token gesture to a sense of public ownership which minimises alienation and vandalism but about creating a dialogue from which people can gain a real understanding of the artist's aims and themselves contribute to the critical debate.

Peter Fink says: "I use public consultation of various kinds to test the initial degree of openness to my ideas and general perceptions, not as a way of trying to reach an aesthetic endorsement but as a way of helping me to understand the sort of issues that my self-formulated starting brief should incorporate."

For Fink's commission at Newport Borough Council, Chief Architect Bernard Wyld describes what consultative processes were used. "Full planning permission was granted after extensive public consultation, during which Peter presented the model and a question-

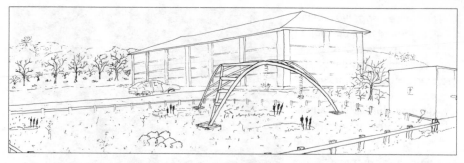

Adam Reynolds' **drawing for a landmark at the Spastics Society's Redditch office**

In 1991 this society established Artists First, a commissioning agency dedicated to creating opportunities for artists with disabilities, with its offices in Cardiff, Redditch, Huntingdon, Wakefield, Bristol and Crawley providing the first sites. Open or limited competitions are used to select artists who may work singly or collaboratively, with the agency providing special equipment and personnel back-up where needed. A register of artists is also being compiled.

and-answer display in the form of a travelling exhibition. Venues including Sainsbury's supermarket, leisure centres, building societies, libraries and the local art gallery. About 30,000 people saw the proposal and a survey of written comments revealed a surprising ratio of 3:1 in favour. Equally surprising was the positive attitude of the local press throughout the project."

Reaching people

When an artwork is to be sited in a place in which people live, work or spend their leisure time, those people have to be consulted. A problem this poses is that while many individuals neatly package themselves (or can be packaged) into 'consultable' units, most do not.

Artists are encouraged to consult with defined groups, whether through workshops or presentations. Children are consulted through schools, young people through youth clubs, elderly people through residential homes. Often the views of the majority slip through the net – men and women who go out of the area to work, unemployed people who don't use designated centres, older people who live in their own homes and parents at home with young children.

For Jan Dungey of the Company of Imagination, "the most effective way of gaining people's interest is by talking to them. In shops, pubs, in their homes and wherever they meet. There is no replacement for face-to-face communication! Talking to people and them hearing about what you're doing by word-of-mouth is worth all the bits of paper pushed through doors."

Adam Reynolds believes direct communication – face-to-face conversation – may have allayed negative responses from staff working at the Spastics Society offices in Redditch to his designs for internal and

Margaret Benyon's *Solar Markers,* 4 x 2.5cm holograms on glass, mounted on rocks in Canberra, Australia. Photo: the artist

"Made in Australia where there is direct sunlight almost every day and people spend much of their spare time outdoors, I used the outdoor culture of Australia as source material. Hologram fragments showing underwater elements, coral and shells (water) were mounted to burnt rocks (fire and earth) taken from a barbecue, and taken outside to be lit by direct sun as part of the piece. They were inscribed with the words 'hot', 'wet', 'dry' and 'cold', pointing to the geology of the rocks and the proto-science years when earth, fire and water were the elements. The 'light' image of the hologram appears to be inside the 'heavy' rock, each intended as a small universe to be held in the hand, to be exchanged with work by other artists and used in the Australian bush as an Aboriginal might mark the path of the sun with rocks. Some were left in the Australian bush for people to stumble across. One of the most interesting aspects of this work was that it seemed to by-pass monetary value systems. Initially made as exchange pieces, three were also bought by the Museum of Holography in New York."

external artwork. On his preliminary visits, people were intrigued by his idea for linking the interior of the new building to its site. His proposal involved featuring an existing newt pond by creating a newt for each staff member and working with them to locate the creatures around the building.

Maquettes for the external bridge structure and internal decoration were left at the offices with a comment book for staff. The disparity between verbal and written responses was striking. Written concerns focused on art taking money away from a financially constrained organisation and the safety of the bridge for children, and also on the negative connotation attached to newts! Had the comments arisen in conversation, Reynolds would have been able to explain that money wasn't coming from Spastic Society funds and the bridge structure would make an unattractive 'climbing frame' because of its size.

His experience has led him to question the primacy of the written word as a method of eliciting reactions. "Leaving the maquette alongside the comments book was like saying OK, tell me what's wrong with it." While he has taken on board many of the comments, his real ambition is to get back on site and work with people directly so they can achieve a mutually agreed end-product.

Checklist

- Clarify at the beginning who will be responsible for consultation, with whom and on what. Avoid being blocked half way through the process because somebody wants a public enquiry.

Judith Cowan's *Touching Earth and Sky* in bronze sited on the Chiltern Sculpture Trail in 1991.
Photo: Oxford Sculpture Project

This artist-led organisation formed in 1989 created the Chiltern Sculpture Trail on Forestry Commission land 20 miles from Oxford. So far, 13 commissioned works, funded by Southern Arts and Oxfordshire County Council, have been sited. The only artist-led sculpture trail in the country, the intention is to move away from traditional materials such as wood and stone and commission work which is more experimental and challenges notions of what might be acceptable in a rural outdoor location.

- Keep talking to people. Initiate requests for meetings, project updates and try to show visually as well as verbally what you're up to.
- If you are responsible for consulting the public, make sure resources have been allowed for you to do so.
- Remember 'the public' do not gather in one place at one time. Go to shops, pubs, factories, use existing networks such as clubs, political groups and Women's Institute meetings as well as schools, hospitals, homes and so on.
- If public workshops are planned to get people involved, facilities have to be provided which are accessible to people who are disabled and non disabled, and consideration given to childcare and transport. All have financial implications and costs need including in a budget.
- Don't rely on a 'comments book'! Talk to people and engage their interest.

Attractions

For artists taking on commissions, the attractions appear to be greater than the final cheque! Working with a site, with a community, being part of a team, pitting themselves against a challenge, widening access to art – each or many of these tempt artists to make work outside the gallery.

But the main attraction is that any of these factors can affect the final artwork in exciting and unexpected ways. As Kate Russell says: "The aspect of working collaboratively which most inspires me is the ever present potential for surprises – to discover something which may initially show up as a problem which expands and somehow releases image or idea. Breakthroughs in technique, philosophy or approach seem more possible and probable in these ventures."

9 • Further reading

This listing contains details of books, catalogues, reports, magazines and selected articles which provide further insights into contemporary art in public settings. Although distribution sources have been indicated where possible, some publications are available from art libraries. It would be advisable however to check availability, price and postage costs if you plan to buy any by mail-order.

Publications

A New London, Richard Rogers and Mark Fisher, Penguin, 1992, ISBN 01 401579 4 8 . A vision for the regeneration London, including discussion on how to develop urbanism in the capital's public spaces. Available at £8.99.

A New Necessity, Tyne International, 1990, ISBN 0 9516057 0 4. Catalogue for the First Tyne International curated by Declan McGonagle in which artists defined 'public' art. Available from Tyne International, 6 Higham Place, Newcastle upon Tyne NE1 8AF tel 091 230 2891.

A Planning Study for Seattle Art in the Civic Context, Hirchfield and Rouch, Seattle Arts Commission, 1984.

A Sense of Place, ed Peter Davies/Tony Knipe, Ceolfrith Press, 1984. Looks at sculpture internationally with a section on sculptures commissioned for Grizedale Forest. Out of print but copies may be available in art libraries.

A Space for Dreaming – a different reality, Bede Gallery, 1991. Book on the work of sculptor Richard Harris published to co-incide with an exhibition. Available at £11.15 inc p&p from Bede Gallery, Butcher's Bridge Road, Jarrow, Tyne & Wear NE32 5QA.

Alchemy – the public art programme at the Garden Festival Wales, ed Maggie Gilson, Garden Festival Wales, 1992, ISBN 0 951390 0 9. Illustrated catalogue with foreword by the organisers. Available at £2 from Garden Festival Wales Visual Arts Unit, Victoria, Ebbw Vale, Gwent NP3 6UF tel 0495 350010.

Art and Mental Health Hospitals, ed Malcolm Miles, British Health Care Arts Centre. Articles on artists in residence schemes and advice on setting up arts projects in hospitals. Available from British Health Care Arts, Duncan of Jordanstone College of Art, Perth Road, Dundee DD1 4HT tel 0382 23261.

Art at Broadgate, Rosehaugh Stanhope Developments plc, 1992. Introduction by Marina Vaizey with illustrations and texts on permanently sited works at Broadgate, London.

Art at Work in Milton Keynes, Milton Keynes Development Corporation, 1990. Giving location of artworks and works in progress with full-colour illustrations.

Art & Craft in Green Places, Sara Grant Thorold, Southern Arts/Hampshire Gardens Trust, 1992. Looks at the use of art and craft work in the landscape and examples of good practice. Available at £6 inc p&p from Southern Arts, 13 St Clements Street, Winchester SO23 9UQ.

Art & Craft Works – a step-by-step guide, Southern Arts, ISBN 0 9501228 4 X. Contains case studies from the Southern Arts region and commission contract checklist. Available at £5.50 from Southern Arts, 13 St Clements Street, Winchester SO23 9DQ.

Art for Architecture, ed Deanna Petherbridge, HMSO, ISBN 0 11 751794 1. Subtitled a handbook for commissioning, covers art in architecture with examples from this country and abroad; commissioning models including one for artists' initiatives; guidelines on commissioning for all parties; bibliography and sample contract. Out of print, but may be available in art libraries.

Art for Public Places, Malcolm Miles, Winchester Press, 1989, ISBN 0 95067838 4. Discusses the context for public art projects in the UK, USA and Eastern Europe. Available from Winchester School of Art, Park Lane, Winchester, Hants SO23 8DL.

9 • Further reading

Art & Healthcare, Linda Moss, DSS Health Building Directorate, 1989, ISBN 185195. Intended for artists and organisations, shows how the arts work for hospitals, covering how schemes are set up and funded, and case studies including artists in residence schemes. Available at £6.

Art in Hospitals, Lesley Greene, The King's Fund, 1989, ISBN 1 85551 046 4. Full-colour illustrated guide and accompanying video on the commissioning of work for healthcare settings, with examples and practical information. Available at £15 from 14 Palace Court, London W2 4HT.

Art in Public Places, John Beardsley, Partners for Livable Places, 1987. Survey of USA projects supported by the National Endowment for the Arts. Available from Partners for Livable Places, 1429 21st Street NW, Washington DC 20036, USA.

Art in the urban environment, Roland Miller, Public Arts, 1988. Report commissioned by Thamesdown Borough Council from Public Arts. Available from Public Arts, 24 Bond Street, Wakefield WF1 2QP.

Art into Landscape, Arts Council, 1974. Catalogue from the Serpentine Gallery exhibition of some of the proposals generated by a national competion organised by the Arts Council, RIBA, the Institute of Landscape Architects and the Sunday Times to make work for open spaces.

Art within Reach, ed Peter Townsend, Art Monthly and Thames & Hudson, ISBN 0 500 97315 6. Covers the implications of artists working in the public arena with details of contractual arrangements and legal and copyright considerations. Available at £6.95 from Out of print but may be held in art libraries.

Artists Worlds • Mundos Articos, Edge Biennale Trust, 1992. Documentation of the 1992 Edge commissioned events in London and Madrid.

Arts and the changing city an agenda for urban regeneration, Biish American Arts Association, 1989, ISBN 0 951 4763 00. Report on a conference which focused on arts and urban regeneration. Available from BBAA, 116 Commercial Street, London E1 tel 071 247 5385.

Arts in Healthcare in the Northern Region, ed Helen Payne, Northern Arts Board, 1992. Looks at residencies and commissions in health care settings in the region, as well as resources, organisations and services which may help in the development of new projects. Available from Northern Arts Board, 9/10 Osborne Terrace, Newcastle upon Tyne NE2 1NZ tel 091 282 6334.

Being and Circumstance Notes Towards a Conditional Art, Robert Irwin, Lapis Press, 1985.

Bellgrove, Alan Dunn, 1990, ISBN 0 951 8551 0 7. Doccumentation of 15 posterworks by 17 artists at Bellgrove Station, Glasgow and three related essays. Available at £4.50 inc p&p from Bellgrove Station Billboard Project, 27A North Hamilton Street, Kilmarnock KA1 2QL tel 0563 72086.

Blame God Billboard Projects, ICA/Artangel/Orchard Gallery, 1986, ISBN 0 905263 60 X. Illustrated book about Les Levine's billboard project in London, Dublin and Derry and the controversy generated. Available from ICA, The Mall, London SW1.

Commissioned Art and Professional Practice, Brighton Polytechnic Media Services, 1992, ISBN 1 871966 167. Handbook to accompany a study video on Brendan Neiland whose work has been commissioned by British Rail, with articles by Marina Vaizey, Jane Priestman, William Packer, Reinhard Rudolph and the artist. Available from Media Services, Brighton Polytechnic, Mouslecoomb, Brighton BN2 4GJ.

Commissions and Collaborations, Mills & Allen, 1992. Illustrated brochure published in conjunction with the BBC and Radio Times documenting the BBC Billboard Art Project in May 1992.

Confrontations, Laing Art Gallery, 1987. Includes discussion of the work of Dennis de Groot and Ddart. Available from Laing Art Gallery, Higham Place, Newcastle upon Tyne NE 1 8AG tel 091 232 7734.

Context & Collaboration – the international public art symposium, Public Art Commissions Agency, 1992. Report on the 1990 symposium with contributions from architects, designers and artists including Kathryn Gustafson, Tess Jaray, Conrad Atkinson, Antoni Miralda and Ian Ritchie. Available from PACA, Studio 6, Victoria Works, Vittoria Street, Birmingham B1 3PE tel 021 212 4454.

Dudley Metropolitan Borough Public Art Guide, John Bennett, Dudley MBC, 1990, ISBN 0900911 27 1. Full colour catalogue of the range of historical and contemporary public art works in the borough. Available at £2.50.

Engineers of the Imagination, 2nd edition, Welfare State International, 1990, ISBN 0 413 52800 6. Practical guide to creating processions, large-scale puppets and sculptures, fixed structures, fire and ice technology, shadow puppets, processional theatre and dance music and celebratory food and feasts. Available at £8.95 from AN Publications, PO Box 23, Sunderland SR4 6DG. Tel 091 514 3600.

Environmental Design Quality in Health Care, Peter Scher, Arts for Health. A discussion paper. Available at £10 inc p&p from Arts for Health, Manchester Polytechnic, All Saints, Manchester M15 6BY.

Fact Pack 2 Slide Indexes, Susan Jones, AN Publications. Listing 36 indexes and registers nationally, some open to application. Available at £1.85 from AN Publications, PO Box 23, Sunderland SR4 6DG tel 091 456 3589.

Festival Landmarks '90, Gateshead Garden Festival, 1990. Catalogue of the art, craft poetry and performance art at the Gateshead Garden Festival. Available at £5.50 inc p&p from Public Art Development Trust, 1A Cobham Mews, Agar Street, London NW1 9SB.

Going Public a field guide to developments in art in public places, Jeffrey L Cruikshank & Pam Korza, AES Publications, 1988. Practical manual describing commissioning processes and administration of public art projects, includes resources lists and case studies. Available at $19.95 from Arts Extension Service, Division of Continuing Education, University of Massachusetts, Amherts, MA 01003, USA.

In Through the Front Door, Jayne Earnscliffe, Arts Council, 1992. Examples of good practice in visual arts and disability, with a section on art in public. Available at £10.95 (inc p&p) from AN Publications, PO Box 23, Sunderland SR4 6DG tel 091 567 3589.

Insights on Sites Perspectives on Art in Public Places, ed Stacey Paleologus Harris, Parners for Livable Places, 1984. Available from Partners for Livable Places, 1429 21st Street NW, Washington DC 20036, USA.

Introduction to the Thoughts and Deeds of Common Ground, ed Angela King/Sue Clifford, Common Ground, 1990. The 1990 report of the organisation's work covering Parish Maps, New Milestones and other projects. Available from 45 Shelton Street, London WC2H 9HJ tel 071 379 3109.

L'art et La Ville, SKIRA & Secrétariat Genéral des Ville Nouvelles. Town planning and contemporary art in French new towns. Available from Le Conseiller pour les Arts Plastiques, Groupe Central des Villes Nouvelles, 21 rue Moillis, Bâtiment C, 75015 Paris, France.

Large-scale photography in public settings, ed Philippa Goodall & Kate Green, Photo Call, 1993. Research has been completed on this publication, for publication date contact Photo Call, MAC, Cannon Hill Park, Birmingham B12 9QH tel 021 446 5086 .

Les Dossiers d'Art Public No6, ed Hervé Bechy, Art Public Promotion, 1991. Report on a public art symposium held at the Museum of Modern Art Paris in October 1990, giving examples from UK, Europe and USA. Available at £15 inc p&p from Art Public Promotion, 71 rue d'Hautpoul, 75019, Paris, France.

Living Proof views of a world living with HIV & AIDS, ed Jenny Barnett, Artists' Agency, 1992, ISBN 09509797 2 4. Compilation of work by people affected by HIV and AIDS and work by writer Michael McMillan and photographer Nicholas Lowe resulting from a year-long residency in the North East. Available at £10 plus postage £1.50 from Artists' Agency, 18 Norfolk Street, Sunderland SR1 1EA.

Lux Europae, 1992. Catalogue to accompany an exhibition in 1992 of sculptures and installations by British and EC artists on the theme of light and celebration. Available from 22 Dublin Street, Edinburgh EH1 3PP tel 031 557 6464.

Making Ways, 3rd edition, ed D Butler, AN Publications, 1989, ISBN 0 907730 16 7. Includes chapters on working to commission, as an artist in residence and planning and fundraising for projects. Available at £11.99 inc p&p from AN Publications, PO Box 23, Sunderland SR4 6DG.

Memorials by Artists, Harriet Frazer, Harriet Frazer, 1990. A booklet on the history of the art of memorial design to accompany a register of artists and makers working in stone who can be commissioned to make public or private memorials. Available at £3 inc p&p from Snape Priory, Saxmundham, Suffolk IP17 1SA tel 0728 88 8934.

Mosaic as Art, Jane Muir, Vidian, 1992. A 54-minute video film covering the design and making of mosaic panels and murals from artist Jane Muir's viewpoint. Available at £23 ex p&p from Vidian, 9 Parson's Mead, East Molesey, Surrey KY8 9DT tel 081 979 9977.

Mural Manual, 2nd edition, Carol Kenna & Steve Lobb, Greenwich Mural Workshop, 1991, ISBN 0 907730 03 5. Covers the practicalities of setting up mural projects. Available at £5.40 inc p&p from AN Publications, PO Box 23, Sunderland SR4 6DG.

New Milestones - Sculpture, Community and the Land, Joanna Morland, Common Ground, 1988, ISBN 1 870364 03 1. Describes six 'New Milestones' sculpture commissions, with practical information and essay on how human activity has shaped and punctuated the landscape. Available at £5.95 inc p&p from Common Ground, 45 Shelton Street, London WC2H 9HJ tel 071 379 3109.

Out of Town, Community Council of Lincolnshire, 1990, ISBN 0 9515688 0 9. Report on an East of England Conference on arts in rural areas. Available at £5 inc p&p from Community Council of Lincolnshire, 1 Kesteven Street, Sleaford, Lincs NG34 7DT.

Partners, Arts Council, 1992. Partners 1 & 2 cover the practical considerations of being an artist in residence in educational settings. Available at £2.50

9 • Further reading

each from Arts Council Education Department, 14 Great Peter Street, London SW1T 3NQ tel 071 33 0100.

Percent for Art a review, Phyllida Shaw, Arts Council, 1991, ISBN 07287 0628 8. Examines projects in the USA, Europe and the UK, and offers recommendations for the future implementation of percent for art here. Available at £11 inc p&p from AN Publications PO Box 23, Sunderland SR4 6DG.

Register of Artists & Craftsmen in Architecture, 2nd edition, Theo Crosby and Sharon Kirwan, Art & Architecture Ltd, 1989. Illustrated examples and other information on 48 members' work and draft code of practice for art and architecture. Available from Art & Architecture, Dunsdale, Forest Row, East Sussex RH18 5BD.

Residencies in Education – Setting them up and making them work, Daniel Dahl, ed Susan Jones, AN Publications, 1990, ISBN 0 907730 09 4. Case-studies and information section covering contracts, insurance, health & safety, training, resources, rates of pay for artists and funding prospects. Available at £7.25 inc p&p from AN Publications, PO Box 23, Sunderland SR4 6DG tel 091 567 3589.

Ron Haselden – Fête and other works, Hilary Gresty, Serpentine Gallery, 1990, ISBN 1 870814 65 7. Covering how this work developed and containing illustrations of it and related works since 1988. Available from Serpentine Gallery, Kensington Gardens, London W2 3XA.

Spirit of Soho Mural, Freeform Arts Trust & Alternative Arts. An illustrated diary of the production of this mural, a collaboration between Freeform Arts Trust and Alternative Arts. Available at £5 from Freeform Arts Trust, 38 Dalston Lane, Hackney, London E8 3AZ.

Strategy for Public Art in Cardiff Bay, Vivien Lovell, Cardiff Bay Development Corporation, 1990. Report by the Public Art Consultancy Team with strategy for including public art in the area's redevelopment. Available at £15 from Cardiff Bay Arts Trust, The Exchange Building, Mount Stuart Square, Cardiff CF1 6EB.

The Arts in Health Care, Judy Berry, Yorkshire Arts Board, 1991, ISBN 0 904659 05 4. Primarily for managers, practical information on how to involve the arts in health care, includes project examples, an article on commissioning artists and lists of local authority departments and other organisations in Yorkshire. Available at £3 inc p&p from Yorkshire Arts Board, 21 Bond Street, Dewsbury, W Yorks WF13 1AX tel 0924 455555.

The Furnished Landscape – applied art in public places, Nuttgens, van den Broeke, Heath, Houston, Bellew Publishing, 1992, ISBN 1 85725 047 8. Book to accompany the Crafts Council exhibition which reviewed the role and potential for applied art within landscape design. Available at £10.50.

The New Deal for Artists, R D McKinzie, Princeton University Press, 1973.

The Public Art Report Local Authority Commissions of Art for Public Places, Phyllida Shaw, Public Art Forum, 1990. Demonstrates local authority commitment to public art with examples drawn from the work of public art agencies and authorities. Available at £5.50 inc p&p from Public Art Development Trust, 1A Cobham Mews, Agar Grove, London NW1 9SB.

The Sculpted Forest, ed Rupert Martin, Redcliffe Press, 1990, ISBN 0 948265 04 3. Documents and illustrates sculptures sited in the Forest of Dean over a five-year period by 16 artists. Available at £7.95 from 49 Park Street, Bristol.

Travelling Hopefully – a Study of the Arts in the Transport System, Naseem Khan and Ken Worpole, Illuminations, 1992. Gives examples in the UK and Sweden and makes recommendations for future practice. Available from Illuminations, 47 Chalton Street, London NW1 1HY tel 071 383 4990.

TSWA 3D, ed Lingwood/Foster/Harvey, TSWA Ltd, 1987, ISBN 0 9506991 5 2. Documents the commissioning and siting of twelve temporary works in nine cities, with an essay by Richard Cork.

TSWA Four Cities Project, ed James Lingwood, TSWA Ltd, 1990. Documentation of artists' works and proposals for Derry, Glasgow, Newcastle and Plymouth and discussions between curators and critics.

Urban Trends 1, Policy Studies Institute, 1992. Looks at the role the arts has played in urban regeneration. Available from Policy Studies Institute, 100 Park Village East, London NW1 3SR tel 071 387 2171.

Visual Arts Information Services Handbook, AXIS, 1992, ISBN 1 897616 007. Lists major sources of information on visual arts, crafts and photography in the UK indicating specialist areas including public art and publications. Includes details of slide indexes and slide borrowing facilities. Available at £3 ind/£4 org inc p&p from AXIS, Leeds Metropolitan University, Calverley Street, Leeds, LS1 3HE, tel 0532 833125.

Articles & Magazines

Art Monthly, monthly magazine. Annual subscription available at £20 indiv from Art Monthly, Suite 17, 26 Charing Cross Road, London WC2M 0DG.

'Percent-for-art', Gary Power, *Art Monthly*, 152 Dec/Jan 92. Looks at how percent for art schemes could be protected, drawing on knowledge of US methods.

Artists Newsletter, AN Publications. Monthly magazine with listings, articles, features and news on all aspects of visual arts, crafts and photography including regular coverage of art in public. Available at £16 individual from AN Publications, PO Box 23, Sunderland SR4 6DG.

'Art and Vandalism', Bill Laws & Steve Lobb, *Artists Newsletter*, April 88. Discusses problems of accidental and deliberate damage to public art works and possible solutions.

'Being part of the process', Brian Baker, *Artists Newsletter*, Sept 92. How artists were involved in Garden Festival Wales.

'Clay and art in the environment', Tanya Harrod, *Artists Newsletter*, July 92. On Kate Malone's public artworks and how ceramics enhances the environment.

'Commissioning for the locality', Malcolm Miles, *Artists Newsletter*, June 89. Examines commissioning practice and the role of art agencies.

'Commissioning the Crafts in Scotland', Malcolm Miles, *Artists Newsletter*, June 90. Looks at the situation in Scotland where commissions are becoming more common.

'I wish I had a town like this', Bernard Wyld, *Artists Newsletter*, Oct 90. Discusses the affect of having Peter Fink as town sculptor at Newport.

'Making it work', Susanna Robinson, *Artists Newsletter*, June 92. Disappointed and disillusioned after working with a public art agency, she calls for a code of practice for public art commissioning.

'Striking at the Heart of Art', Nik Houghton, *Artists Newsletter*, Dec 90. Covers the work of AVI, billboard saboteurs.

'The Artist and the Forester', Marshall Anderson, *Artists Newsletter*, July 92. Looks at the work of the Forestry Commission and how they work with artists.

'The European Dimension', Roland Miller, *Artists Newsletter*, June 91. Report on a public art symposium in Europe.

'The Philadelphian Story', Joanna Griffin, *Artists Newsletter*, March 91. Looks at the promotion and pioneers of public art in Philadelphia.

'Urban Thresholds', Malcolm Miles, *Artists Newsletter*, April 91. Compares public art in the UK and Australia.

'Working with Architects', Andrew Bradford, *Artists Newsletter*, Jan 91. Looks at collaboration, funding and percent for art.

'Working with Architects 1 & 2', Tim Ostler & Steve Field, *Artists Newsletter*, Oct 84 & Feb 85. Looks in detail at the implications of artists and architects working together.

Artlink, Artlink. Quarterly magazine on Australian visual arts. Available at UK $30 airmail from 363 Esplanade, Henley Beach, S Australia 5022.

Art, Architecture, Environment – special issue, *Artlink*, Vol 11 No 4 Summer 91. Articles include art as conservation of the natural and built environment, art as ecology, eco-design, solar design, collaborative design and earth building.

Bazaar, South Asian Arts Forum. Magazine covering all art forms from a South Asian perspective. Available at £10 indiv from 237 Bon Marché Building, 444 Brixton Road, London SW9 8EJ.

'A New Necessity', Declan McGonagle, *Artscribe*, 82 Summer 90. Curator of the first Tyne International discusses art outside the gallery and the exhibition. (Note *Artscribe* is no longer published)

'Invisible Yearnings', Michael Archer, *Artscribe*, 85 Jan/Feb 91. Discusses the TSWA 'Four Cities' project.

Building Design, Construction Ltd. Weekly publication circulated free to architects containing some articles relevant to the commission of works for public spaces and providing an insight into the world of architects and the construction industry. Available at £58 from Morgan Grampian, 30 Calderwood Street, London SE18 6HQ.

'Heaven's Gate', Richard Porch, *Building Design*, 22/11/91. On Swansea City Council's 'Observatory Project' in which architect Robin Cambell included stained glass by David Pearl, sculpture by Robert Conybear, calligraphy by Ieuan Rees and poetry by Nigel Jenkins in a "team assembled to work under the architect's direction."

'Will Kommen in Berlin', *Building Design*, 11/10/91. On the Alsop Störmer proposal for Potzdamer/ Leipziger Platz in Berlin.

CIRCA. Magazine published four a year with articles, reviews and commentary on visual arts in Ireland. Available at UK £14 indiv from 67 Donegall Pass, Belfast BT17 1DR.

'Politics, Patronage & Public Art', David Baggaley, *Circa*, 54 Nov/Dec 90. Are the conditions of meaning in public spaces are suffficiently understood? .

'Putting public art on the agenda', James Odling Smee, *Circa*, 46 July/Aug 89. Covers the controversy surrounding placing permanent sculptures in Ireland.

'TSWA Four Cities Project – Derry 1990', Fionna Barber, *Circa*, 55 Jan/Feb 91. Discusses work by

9 • Further reading

Dennis Adams, Melanie Counsell, Lee Jaffe, Ilya Kabakov, Moira McIver and Nancy Spero.

Crafts, Crafts Council. Bi-monthly magazine with coverage across the crafts, including commissions and work in public. Available at £25 indiv from 44a Pentonville Road, Islington, London N1 9HF.

'A Brighter Prospect', Rose Jennings, *Crafts*, Jul/Aug 92. Looks at functional art in public around the country.

'Hothouse Hybrids', Stephanie Brown, *Crafts*, July/Aug 90. Covering craft work at the Gateshead Garden Festival.

'In Memoriam', Geraldine Rudge, *Crafts*, May/June 90. Looks at the organisation Memorials for Artists which has created a register of lettercutters and stonecarvers who can be commissioned to inscribe gravestones.

Frieze, Bi-monthly magazine. Available at £18 indiv from 21 denmark Street, London WC2H 8NE, tel 071 379 1533

'Fitting Comments', Naomi Salaman, *Frieze*, Summer 91. Discusses the work of AVI who subvert billboard advertising campaigns in London.

'Under the Canary', David Batchelor, *Frieze*, May 92. Discusses the link between visual arts and corporate image, with reference to Canary Wharf's visual arts programme.

Green Book, Green Book Ltd, ISBN 0265 0088. Quarterly review of the visual arts and literature. Available at £3.95 each from 2 Sydney Place, Bath BA2 6NF tel 0225 332527.

'Flowering Tips open air sculpture in the North', David Craig, *Green Book*, 10. Discusses artists' work along the Consett-Sunderland Sustrans cycle path.

'Sculpture in Britain Today', *Green Book*, 1. Special issue, with articles on 'Sculpture in the Environment', Antony Gormley, 'New Milestones' and sculpture parks.

Public Art Review, Forecast Public Artworks. Twice yearly journal covering art in public in the USA and elsewhere. Available at UK $22 airmail from 2324 University Avenue West, Suite 102, St Paul, Minnestota 55114, USA.

Common Ground, John Carson, *Public Art Review*, Spring/Summer 91. Describes the differences in attitude between the work of Common Ground and other organisations.

'Does it Work?', Malcolm Miles, *Public Art Review*, Summer/Fall 92. Cites the real need for evaluation of art in public places, although organisations in the UK which promote public projects are so consumed by the need to raise money that evaluation is a low priority.

'Public Art as Analgesic', Debbie Duffin, *Public Art Review*, Summer/Fall 92. Looks at the work of British Health Care Arts who advises on integrating artworks into health care facilities and involving artists in design teams.

Sculpture, International Sculpture Center. Bi-monthly magazine covering sculpture in the USA and elsewhere with regular listings of members' commissioned works. Available from 1050 Potomac Street NW, Washington DC 20007, USA.

'Abstraction's Whipping Boy', Nancy Princenthal, *Sculpture*, Jan/Feb 90. About Richard Serra's work and its disquieting lack of images.

'Breaking Ground Art in the Environment', Jude Schwendenwien, *Sculpture*, Sept/Oct 89. Looks at the work of leading environmental artists in the USA.

'Percent for Art Up-date', *Sculpture*, Jan/Feb 90. Statistics on which US states are giving money for the arts and how much.

Public Art - special issue, *Sculpture*, May/June 92. Articles include 'Redrawing the Boundaries of Public Art' Gary Apgar, 'Art into Life' Hafthor Yngvason, 'The Point Between' Patricia C Phillips.

'Social Responsibility & Censorship', Eleanor Heartney, *Sculpture*, Jan/Feb 90. By turning its back on social responsibility this critic argues the artworld has made itself vulnerable to attack by the forces of censorship.

'The New Art Furniture', Constance Stapleton, *Sculpture*, July/Aug 90. Looks at the US trend for collectors to commission furniture which challenges the boundaries separating art and crafts.

'What's Missing at Battery Park?', Eleanor Heartney, *Sculpture*, Nov/Dec 89. Looks at issues surrounding the siting art at Battery City Park, New York and questions whether public artworks can be truly successful when placed in a setting that ultimately advances an exclusionary view of community.

10 • Contacts

In this section, an emphasis has been placed on listing groups, projects and organisations who are mentioned in the book as well as others who work in similar ways. However, this cannot be a comprehensive list, and the addresses of individual artists have been excluded to prevent unwelcome attentions.

Artist-led initiatives – which range from informal, occasional collaborations to companies with paid administrative staff. – have been grouped together because they are practice-led, undertaking both the creative and administrative aspects of project generation.

Also listed are organisations concerned with art and environmental issues, public art agencies, sculpture trusts, professional associations, artists' registers, key information services and the arts and crafts councils and regional arts boards. For space reasons we have not been able to include the many local authority departments which encourage and enable the broad spectrum of activities pertinent to this book. The listings of artists' registers and information services contains only those mentioned in the book, more detailed information on these topics being contained in publications listed in **Further Reading.**

Art & environment

Common Ground, 45 Shelton Street, London, WC2H 9HJ, tel: 071 379 3109, contact: Sue Clifford. Through the development of projects which encourage communities to commission sculpture, promotes the importance of cultural heritage, local distinctiveness and links with the past.

Groundwork Foundation, 85-87 Cornwall Street, Birmingham, B3 3BY, tel: 021 236 8565, contact: Information Officer. Has encouraged development of 30 independent Groundwork Trusts dedicated to working in partnership with others to regenerate local environments in places damaged by past industrial activities. Those whose work includes visual arts activities are: *Rossendale Groundwork Trust*, New Hall Hey Road, Rawtenstall, Lancashire, BB4 6HR, tel 0706 211421, fax 0706 210770; *South Leeds Groundwork Trust*, Environment & Business centre, Wesley Street Mill, Wesley Street, Morley, Leeds, LS27 9ED, tel 0532 380601, fax 0532 525057; *St Helens Groundwork Trust*, 19-27 Shaw Street, St Helens, Merseyside WA10 1DN, tel 0744 39396, fax 0744 24081; *Blackburn Groundwork Trust*, Glenfield park (site 2), Blackwater Road, Blackburn BB1 5QH, tel 0254 265163, fax 0254 692835; *West Cumbria Groundwork Trust*, Crowgarth House, 48 High Street, Cleator Moor, Cumbria, CA25 5AA, tel 0946 813677, fax 813059; *Merthyr & Cynon Groundwork Trust*, Fedw Hir, Llwydcoed, Aberdare CF44 0DX, tel 0685 883880, fax 0685 879990; *Wigan Groundwork Trust*, 116 Wigan Road, Ashton-in Makerfield, WN4 9SX, tel 0942 270770, fax 0942 719636; *Black Country Groundwork Trust*, Red House, Hill Lane, Great Barr, Sandwell B43 6ND, tel 021 357 4394, fax 021 358 7045; *Kerrier Groundwork Trust*, Wilson Way, Pool, Redruth, Cornwall TR15 3RS, tel 0209 211364, fax 0209 211301.

Platform, 7 Horsleydown Lane, Tower Bridge, Bermondsey, London, SE1 2LN, tel: 071 403 3738. Interdisciplinary arts and ecology group working with communities and using local materials, artists, writers and others to create site-specific events.

Projects Environment, 11 Higher Downs, Altrincham, WA14 2QL, tel: 061 928 1966, contact: Celia Larner/Ian Hunter. Investigates and develops ways in which artists and others can use creativity to address world urban and rural crises.

Sustrans, 35 King Street, Bristol, BS1 4DZ, tel: 0272 268893, contact: John Grimshaw. Generating cycle paths along disused railway lines, working in partnership with others to commission sculpture as mileposts.

Artist-led groups

AFTER, 804 Manchester Road, Castelton, Rochdale, OL11 3AW, tel: 0706 31834, contact: Paul McLaren/Paul Hayward. Artists for the Environment in Rochdale runs workshops and events with a social, ecological, economic and historical emphasis in the region and elsewhere.

Anticopyright, c/o 70 High Street, Leicester; PO Box 406, Stoke on Trent ST1 6DT; PO Box 368, Cardiff CF2 1SQ; PO Box 5975 Chicago, IL 60680-5975, USA. Distribution network for radical flyposters, encouraging people to think about accepted notions of 'public space'.

Art & Environment, 56 Nightingale Lane, London, SW12 8NY, tel: 071 675 5694, contact: Francis Carr. Network of artists and craftspeople with a broad range of skills working to commission.

Art Space Portsmouth/Aspex Gallery, 27 Brougham Road, Portsmouth, PO5 4PA, tel: 0705 874523. Developed the Gateway City Art Walk project for the European Arts Festival 1992, with 11 artists making large paintings sited on buildings around the city.

Artists Support Peace, c/o Space Studios, Brookmill Road, Deptford, London, SE8, contact: Paul Donnelly/Geoff Staden. Organises events and generates temporary works.

Artonic, Old Tech Building, 87 Preston Road, Brighton, BN1 6AF, tel: 0273 559898, contact: Bruce Williams. Andy Parkin, Bruce Williams and Christopher McHugh work collaboratively and individually.

Arts Resource, 21 Foyle Street, Sunderland, SR1 1LE, tel: 091 510 0916, contact: Deborah Hunter. Generates opportunities for artists and links initiatives with sites, partners or funders. See also Artscape.

Artscape, Arts Resource, 21 Foyle Street, Sunderland, SR1 1LE, tel: 091 510 0916, contact: Annette Davies. Environmental art project managed by Arts Resource commissioning permanent works and temporary events for public sites in the city.

Artscope, 24 Douglas Gardens, Dunston, Gateshead, NE11 9RA, tel: 091 413 5340, contact: Malcolm Smith/Steve Marshall. Generates workshops and artworks which encourage participation in the visual arts. Works with people who are disabled and others who have limited access to mainstream arts activities.

AVI (Active Visual Intervention), tel: 071 738 5119, contact: David/Gavin. Using advertising billboards in London to make visual interventions.

Billboard Project (Birmingham), Birmingham Institute of Art & Design, Margaret Street, Birmingham, B3 3BX, tel: 021 331 5966, fax: 021 236 0458, contact: Graham Fagan. Enables artists, writers, community groups and others to design billboards on the Snowhill Queensway in Birmingham's city centre.

Birmingham Arts Trust, Midlands Arts Centre, Cannon Hill Park, Birmingham, B12 9QH, tel: 021 446 4672. Raise the profile of fine artists in the West Midlands by instigating events and developing of studio space.

Bristol Women's Photography Group, c/o 17 Church Path Road, Pill, Bristol, BS20 0EE, tel: 0272 227158, contact: Liz Milner. Developed the 'Billbroads' project as part of the International Women's Festival in Bristol in 1992.

Chrysalis Arts, Old Council Depot, Eshton Road, Gargrave, N Yorks, BD23 3SE, tel: 0756 748042, contact: Rick Faulkner, Kate Maddison. Undertakes commissions for permanent and temporary visual arts projects, celebratory events and street theatre.

Company of Imagination, PO Box 328, Hethersett, Norfolk, NR9 3PU, tel: 0603 507197. Multi-artform group linking art and the environment and working in rural communities.

Dundee Public Arts Programme, Seagate Gallery, 36-40 Seagate, Dundee, DD1 2EJ, tel: 0382 26331, contact: Bob McGilvray. Teams of artists, designers, planners, engineers and architects work on projects integrated into schemes to improve the city's environment.

Edinburgh Sculpture Workshop, 78 Albion Road, Edinburgh, EH7 5QZ, tel: 031 661 3839, contact: Co-ordinator. Organised the 'Niches Project', a series of site-specific sculptural assemblies in the walls of Old Calton Cemetery.

Fine Rats International, The Toll House, 115 High Street, Smethwick, B66 1AG, tel: 021 565 0597, contact: Francis Gomila. Francis Gomila, Colin Pearce, Mark Renn and Ivan Smith specialise in putting on noctural events in places of social and architectural significance.

Freeform Arts Trust, 68 Dalston Lane, London, E8 3AZ, tel: 071 249 3394, contact: Martin Goodrich/Barbara Wheeler Early. Committed to helping communities to improve their visual environment through the development of art in public places projects including landscape design and architecture.

Freeform North Tyneside, Fish Quay Design Centre, North Shields, NE30 1JA, tel: 091 259 5143, contact: Richard Broderick. A project of Freeform

Arts Trust London, teams of artists work with the community to improve the urban environment.

Greenwich Mural Workshop, MacBean Centre, MacBean Street, London, SE18 6LW, tel: 081 854 9266, contact: Carol Kenna/Steve Lobb. Generates mural-making projects as well as providing information for artists.

Horse and Bamboo, Foundry Street, Rawtenstall, Rossendale, BB4 6HQ, tel: 0706 220241, contact: Bob Frith. Multi-artform company creating live art performances and temporary events based on an annual horse-drawn tour around rural areas.

House Artists' Co-op, Tottenham Green Co-op Workshops, Unit 5, 2 Somerset Road, London, N17 9EJ, tel: 081 808 4790, contact: Lawrence Sullivan. Undertakes commissions for works in public and community locations.

Hull Time Based Arts, 6 Posterngate, Hull, HU1 2JN, tel: 0482 216446, contact: Mike Stubbs. Commissions and promotes live art and temporary installations in public settings.

Islington Schools Environmental Project, Robert Blair School, Brewery Road, London, N7 9BL, tel: 071 700 4565, contact: David Stone. Arts education group using residencies and workshops to carry out environmental improvements in Islington schools.

Open Hand Studios, 571 Oxford Road, Reading, Berks, RG3 1HL, tel: 0734 597752, contact: Jenny Eadon. Jenny Eadon and Arthur op den Brouw created the Forbury Lion for Reading Art Week 1992. Other artists in the studios work on temporary and permanent commissions.

Oxford Sculpture Project, PO Box 452, Oxford, OX4 1GU, tel: 0865 819477, contact: Jacqui Mansfield. Formed by sculptors to increase opportunities for artists, developed the Chiltern Sculpture Trail through a programme of residencies and commissions.

Partnership Arts, Providence Mill, Alexandra Street, Hyde, Cheshire, SK14 1DX, tel: 061 367 8640, contact: Terry Eaton. Generates temporary and permanent commissions in the North West and elsewhere for public and private clients.

Public Art Resource Unit, Harvington House, Parsons Street, Dudley, DY1 1HZ, tel: 0384 236887, contact: Steve Field. Borough artist Steve Field generates commission opportunities and provides advice and information.

Raku Works, Mercer House, Mercer Park, Clayton-le-Moors, Accrington, BB5 5NZ, tel: 0254 391412, contact: Mags Casey. Runs projects which involve a high degree of community input to the design and making of ceramic sculptures for public places.

Site Insite, Meadowmill Studios, West Hendersons Wynd, Dundee, 0382 22124, contact: Chris Kelly/Chris Biddlecombe. Undertake commissions in the community which are concerned with the sympathetic and sensitive development of urban space.

St Peter's Riverside Project, c/o Artists Agency, 18 Norfolk Street, Sunderland, SR1 1EA, tel: 091 510 9318, contact: Colin Wilbourn. Artist/consultant developing opportunities for his own and other artists' work as part of a re-development programme.

Start Studios, High Elms, Upper Park Road, Victoria Park, Manchester, M14 5RU, tel: 061 276 6345, contact: Jack Sutton. Start Out undertakes community environmental art projects for sites outside hospitals in Manchester and creates opportunities for members and artists to undertake paid work in community settings.

The Art of Change, Level 3, Lion Court, 435 The Highway, Wapping, London, E1 9HT, tel: 071 702 8802, fax: 071 702 8803, contact: Peter Dunn. Formerly the Docklands Community Poster Project, work includes projects which enable communities to communicate their concerns and which raise awareness of their environment.

The Pioneers, Old Library, The Hayes, Cardiff, CF1 2DQ, tel: 0222 222933, contact: Nick Clements. Generates commissions and residencies with communities in South Wales.

Those Environmental Artists, 96 Bramhall Lane South, Bramhall, Cheshire, SK7 2EA, tel: 061 439 1149, contact: Val Murray. Val Murray, Lynn Pilling, Jon Biddulph and Peter Hatton collaborate on temporary commissions and events for public sites and also work individually.

Welfare State International, The Ellers, Ulverston, Cumbria, LA12 0AA, tel: 0229 581127, contact: Sue Gill. Multi-artform company specialising in celebratory events and other temporary manifestations.

Whitstable Artists & Musicians Collective, c/o 15 Norman Road, Whitstable, Kent, CT5 4JY, tel: 0227 276534, contact: Nigel Hobbins. Developed the sea benches project between 1989-92. Artists now developing individual commissioned work.

Artists' registers

African & Asian Visual Artists Archive, The Coach House Small Business Centre, 2 Upper York Street, St Paul's, Bristol, BS2 8QN, tel: 0272 244492. Largest most comprehensive archive and register of African and Asian artists' work in Britain.

Also supplies slides to the Women of Colour index at the Women Artists Slide Library.

Memorials by Artists, Snape Priory, Saxmundham, Suffolk, IP17 1SA, tel: 0728 88 8934, contact: Harriet Frazer. Register of artists and makers who can work to commission on memorials for public and private places which is used to link client and artist. Can facilitate the selection, planning and fixing of the memorial.

Panchayat, 8 Hoxton St, London, N1 6NG, tel: 071 729 6273, contact: Shaheen Merali. Arts and education resource holding information on South Asian artists.

Women Artists Slide Library, Fulham PalaceBishop's Avenue, London, SW6 6EA, tel: 071 731 7618. Contains over 19,000 slides as well as catalogues, reports, magazines and other published material on women artists. Has a section on Black women artists' work.

Arts councils & boards

Arts Council, 14 Great Peter Street, London, SW1P 3NQ, tel: 071 333 0100.

Irish Arts Council, 70 Merrion Square, Dublin, 2, tel: (010 353) 611840.

Arts Council of Northern Ireland, 81A Stranmillis Road, Belfast, BT9 5DU, tel: 0232 381 591. Funded by the Office of Northern Ireland, rather than through the Arts Council route.

Crafts Council, 44a Pentonville Road, Islington, London, N1 9HF, tel: 071 278 7700.

Crafts Council of Ireland, The Powers Court, Town House Centre, South William Street, Dublin, 2, tel: (010 353) 1611840.

East Midlands Arts Board, Mountfields House, Forest Road, Loughborough, LE11 3HU, tel: 0509 218292. Covers Leicestershire, Nottinghamshire, Northamptonshire and Derbyshire except the High Peak District

Eastern Arts Board, Cherry Hinton Hall, Cherry Hinton Road, Cambridge, CB1 4DW, tel: 0223 215355. Covers Bedfordshire, Cambridge, Essex, Hertfordshire, Lincolnshire, Norfolk, Sussex

London Arts Board, Elme House, 133 Long Acre, London, WC2E 9AF, tel: 071 240 1313. Covers Greater London area

North Wales Arts Association, 10 Wellfield House, Bangor, Gwynedd, LL57 1ER, tel: 0248 353248. Covers Clwyd, Gwynedd and the Montgomery district of Powys

North West Arts Board , 4th Floor, 12 Harter Street, Manchester, M1 6HY, tel: 061 228 3062.

Covers Cheshire, Greater Manchester, Lancashire, Merseyside and the High Peak area of Derbyshire

Northern Arts Board, 10 Osborne Terrace, Newcastle upon Tyne, NE2 1NZ, tel: 091 281 6334. Covers Cleveland, Cumbria, Durham, Northumberland, Tyne & Wear

Scottish Arts Council, 12 Manor Place, Edinburgh, EH3 7DO, tel: 031 226 6051. Covers Scotland

South East Arts Board, 10 Mount Ephraim, Tunbridge Wells, TN4 8AS, tel: 0892 515210. Covers Kent, Surrey and East & West Sussex, excluding Greater London areas

South East Wales Arts Association, Victoria Street, Cwmbran, NP44 3YT, tel: 0633 875075. Covers Mid-Glamorgan, South Glamorgan, Gwent and South Powys

South West Arts Board, Bradninch Place, Gandy Street, Exeter, EX4 3LS, tel: 0392 218188. Covers Avon, Cornwall, Devon and Dorset, except Bournemouth, Christchurch and Poole areas of Dorset, Gloucestershire and Somerset

Southern Arts Board, 13 St Clements Street, Winchester, SO23 9UQ, tel: 0962 855099. Covers Berkshire, Buckinghamshire, Hampshire, Isle of Wight, Oxfordshire, Wiltshire and the Poole, Bournemouth and Christchurch areas of Dorset

Welsh Arts Council, Museum Place, Cardiff, CF1 3NX, tel: 0222 394 711.

West Midlands Arts Board, 82 Granville Street, Birmingham, B1 2LH, tel: 021 631 3121. Covers Hereford & Worcester, Shropshire, Staffordshire, Warwickshire, West Midlands

West Wales Arts Association, 3 Red Street, Carmarthen, Dyfed, SA31 1QL, tel: 0267 234248. Covers West Glamorgan and Dyfed

Yorkshire and Humberside Arts Board, 21 Bond Street, Dewsbury, WF13 1AX, tel: 0924 455555, fax: 0924 466522. Covers Humberside and North, South & West Yorkshire

Information services

AN Information, PO Box 23, Sunderland, SR4 6DG, tel: 091 567 3589. Provides database print-outs, listings and other information on aspects of the visual arts including art in public.

Arts for Health, Manchester Polytechnic, All Saints, Manchester, M15 6BY, tel: 061 236 8916. Gives advice and information on health care arts projects. Publishes *Artery* magazine.

AXIS – Visual arts information service, Leeds Metropolitan University, Calverley Street, Leeds, LS1 3HE, tel: 0532 833125, contact: Yvonne Deane.

Independent information resource on visual arts practice, developing the National Artists Register as a multi-media image database in 1993.

Professional associations

Art & Architecture, 19 Percy Circus, London, WC1X 9ES. Holds a database of members and publishes an illustrated directory of members' work.

Landscape Institute, 12 Carlton House Terrace, London, SW1, tel: 071 839 4044.

National Artists Association, Membership Secretary, 12 Brookside Terrace, Sunderland, SR2 7RN. Representative body for visual artists, works to improve the economic and social status of artists. A Code of Practice for the visual arts is being researched and NAA is working with Northern Arts Board to develop an Artists' Charter for 1996.

Public Art Forum, Flat 1, The Priory, Webber St, London, SE1 0RQ, tel: 071 928 1221, contact: Lisa Harty. Full membership open to public art consultants/agents and other public art officers, others eligible to join as associate members.

Visual Arts and Galleries Association, The Old School, Witcham, Ely, CB6 2LQ, tel: 0353 776356, contact: Hilary Gresty. Welcomes membership from all sectors of the visual arts community including artists.

Public art agencies

Art in Partnership, 233 Cowgate, Edinburgh, EH1 1NQ, tel: 031 225 4463, contact: Robert Breen. Develops public art commissions, providing opportunities for artists in Scotland and elsewhere. Artists can apply to join the slide index.

Artangel Trust, 133 Oxford Street, London, W1R 1TD, tel: 071 434 2887, contact: James Lingwood. Enables and promotes temporary and non-gallery based work which addresses social and political issues. 0171-336-6801

Artists' Agency, 18 Norfolk Street, Sunderland, SR1 1EA, tel: 091 510 9318, contact: Lucy Milton/ Esther Salamon. Runs residencies and placements for artists and other practitioners in a variety of settings in the North of England. Also involved in the development of art in public projects in the region.

Artists First, Spastics Society, 16 Fitzroy Square, London, W1P 5HQ, tel: 071 383 3205, contact: Jayne Earnscliffe. Provides opportunities for artists with disabilities to work on public commissions. Is building a register of artists.

British Health Care Arts Centre, Duncan of Jordanstone College of Art, 13 Perth Road, Dundee,

DD1 4HT, tel: 0382 23261, fax: 0382 27304, contact: Malcolm Miles. Encourages the commissioning of visual arts in healthcare settings using a slide register of artists and projects. Provides an advisory service for health care services.

Cardiff Bay Arts Trust, The Exchange, Mount Stuart Square, Cardiff, CF1 6EB, tel: 0222 488772, contact: Sally Medlyn/Jasia McArdle. Set up by Cardiff Bay Development Corporation to develop public art commissions within South Cardiff.

City Gallery Arts Trust, South Pavilion, ParklandsGreat Linford, Milton Keynes, MK14 5DZ, tel: 0908 606791, contact: Nicola Kennedy. Initiates and manages residencies and public art commissions in public settings.

Cywaith Cymru/Artwork Wales, 2 John Street, Cardiff, CF1 5AE, tel: 0222 489543, contact: Tamara Krikorian/Simon Fenoulhet. Puts art in the environment through commissions, exhibitions and residencies. Holds a slide index of artists.

Public Art Commissions Agency, Studio 6, Victoria Works, Vittoria Street, Birmingham, B1 3PE, tel: 021 212 4454, contact: Vivien Lovell/Geoff Wood. Sets up public art residencies and commissions for private and public organisations. A register of artists is held on computer and artists can apply for inclusion.

Public Art Development Trust, 1A Cobham Mews, Agar Grove, London, NW1 9SB, tel: 071 284 4983, contact: Sandra Percival/Michaela Crimmin. Encourages and initiates public art projects for public and private bodies, developers, architects and individuals.

Public Art Swindon, Joliffe Studio, Wyvern Theatre, Theatre Square, Swindon, SN1 1QJ, contact: Lorraine Cox. Commissioning public art in Thamesdown.

Public Arts, 24 Bond Street, Wakefield, WF1 2QP, tel: 0924 295791, contact: Graham Roberts. Organises public art commissions, residencies and consultancies in Yorkshire, using its databased register of artists to publicise commission opportunities.

Sculpture trusts

Hampshire Sculpture Trust, North Hill Close, Andover Road, Winchester, SO22 6AQ, tel: 0962 846038.

Portland Sculpture Trust, 36 High Street, Fortuneswell, Portland, Dorset, tel: 0305 823489.

Scottish Sculpture Trust, 3 Bank Street, Inverkeithing, Fyfe, KY11 1LR, tel: 0383 412811.

11 • Developing skills

MA courses

MA Theory & Practice of Public Art & Design
Chelsea College of Art & Design (London Institute), Lime Grove, Shepherds Bush, London W12 8EA. Course leader Faye Carey. 2 years part-time

MFA Public Art, Fine Art
Duncan of Jordanstone College of Art, 13 Perth Road, Dundee DD1 4HT, Course leader Ronald Forbes. 45 weeks. Developed from the MPhil in Public Art

MA in Fine Art
Glasgow School of Art, 167 Renfrew Street, Glasgow G3 6RQ. Course leader (Environmental Art) David Harding. 2 years full-time. Environmental art is one of six areas of study on this course.

Interdisciplinary Studies in Art & Architecture
Kent Institute of Art & Design, New Dover Road, Canterbury CT1 3AN. Course leader Andrew Brighton. 48 weeks full-time, 68 weeks part-time

PGDip/MA Art & Architecture
University of East London, Department of Architecture, Holbrook Centre, Holbrook Road, London E11 5 3EA. Course leader Jane Riches. MA full-time 48 weeks, PGDip 2 terms full-time or 2 calendar years part-time

MA Site-specific Sculpture
Wimbledon School of Art, Merton Hall Road, London SW19 3QA. Course leader Vincent Woropay. 2 years part-time

MA Art in Context
University of Sunderland, School of Art & Design, Backhouse Park, Ryhope Road, Sunderland SR2 7EE. Course Leader Brian Thompson. Course awaiting validation

Degree courses

which include public or contextual art as an area of study

BA Art & Design
Bradford & Ilkley Community College, Great Horton Road, Bradford BD7 1AY

BA Fine Art (Critical Fine Art Practice)
Central St Martins (London Institute), 27 Long Acre, London WC2 9LA

BA Design (Mural Design/Design for Architectural Spaces)
Chelsea College of Art & Design, Manresa Road, London SW3 6LS

BA Fine Art
Coventry University, School of Art & Design, Gosford Street, Coventry

BA Fine Art
Kent Institute of Art & Design, New Dover Road, Canterbury CT1 3AN

BA Visual Art
Lancaster University, Lonsdale Hall, Bailrigg, Lancaster LA1 4YW

BA Fine Art
Lancashire Polytechnic, Victoria Building, Preston PR1 2TQ

HND Design (Architectural Glass)
N E Wales Institute, Clwyd College of Art & Design Technology, Grove Park Road, Wrexham, Clywd LL12 7AA

BA Contemporary Art Practice and BA Fine Art
University of Northumbria at Newcastle, Squires Building, Newcastle upon Tyne NE1 8ST

BA Fine Art
University of Sunderland, School of Art & Design, Backhouse Park, Ryhope Road, Sunderland SR2 7EE

BA Art & Social Context
University of West of England, Faculty of Art, Media & Design, Clanage Road, Bower Ashton, Bristol BS3 2JU

BA Fine Art
Winchester School of Art, Park Avenue, Winchester SO23 8DL

12 • Contributors

Conrad Atkinson is an artist and was a member of the Arts Council's Percent for Art Steering Group. He is currently Chair of Fine Art at the University of California, USA.

Sara Selwood is Director of the visual arts education organisation Art & Society and is currently Associate Research Fellow at the Policy Studies Institute, undertaking a 15-month study into the benefits of public art.

James Peto managed 'A New Necessity', the first Tyne International exhibition, and is now working on the second Tyne International to be held in 1993.

Brian Baker is a free-lance journalist writing for *Building Design, Surveyor, Artists Newsletter, Stage & Television Today, Arts Management Weekly, Museums Journal* and *Public Service Local Government*.

Paul Swales worked with Omega 2 before becoming Public Art Officer for Sheffield City Council in 1991. He has written for this book in a personal capacity.

Yvonne Deane is Director of AXIS – Visual Arts Information Service established in 1991 as an independent resource on the visual arts including art in public.

Jeni Walwin is an independent arts consultant and Arts Development Consultant to Broadgate Estates.

Eddie Chambers, formerly Director of the African & Asian Artists Archive, is now a free-lance curator associated with the Institute of New International Visual Arts.

Lee Corner is a free-lance writer and researcher in the arts working for local authorities, Arts Council and regional arts boards.

Susan Jones is an artist. She also undertakes visual arts research for regional arts boards, the Arts Council, the Arts & Entertainment Training Council and AN Publications. Since 1987, she has been News Editor of *Artists Newsletter*.

Jayne Earnscliffe, artist and free-lance consultant and researcher specialising in advising arts organisations on access, training and programming for people who are disabled, manages Artists First, the public agency which generates commission opportunities for artists with disabilities. *In through the front door*, her book providing examples of good practice in the visual arts for disabled people was published by the Arts Council in 1992.

Barbara Taylor is a consultant and exhibition organiser specialising in the crafts.

Philippa Goodall and **Kate Green** of Photo Call, the Birmingham-based photography organisation, have been undertaking research into the commissioning of large-scale photography works for public settings.

13 • Index

Numbers in italics refer to page number of illustration
Entries in italic indicate titles of works

440 Lights 121

A

ABSA 21
African and Asian Visual Artists Archive 112, 113, 117, 120
agencies and agents 15, 45, 48, 63-4, 79, 80, 81, 86, 112, 115, 136; artist-run 80; for disabled artists 142; feedback from 83
Alexander, Keith *56*, 57
Alsop, Will 106, *107*
animated trails *141*
Antonelli, Karen 86
An Urban Renaissance campaign 16
applications 78-9, 129-30; contents checklist 85-6; empowerment 116- 17; preparation and research for 84-5; quality of presentation 86, 89, 117, 128; responses to a brief 119-20; supporting material 90-1
apprenticeships 49-50
architects: dealing with administration 80; relationships with artists 33, 45-6, 51, 59, 60, 65, 66, 70, 73, 103-6, 111, 128, 132, 133, 140
art agencies *see* agencies and agents
Art and Architecture Group 104
Art of Change 35
artists/consultants *see* consultants/artists
Artists First 142
Artonic *72*
art for places 65, 66, 67, 70, 71, 77, 111
Art in Public Places policy 15, 25
arts boards *see* regional arts boards
Artschwager, Richard *22*
Arts Council policy 15-16, 17-20, 22, 25, 99, 103; 'Arts 2000' 16; Education Dept fact pack 85; funding 15-16, 102; 'New Collaborations' scheme 135; *see also* percent for art
Arts Resource 51
Artworks Wales/Cywaith Cymru 50, 115
Asian artists 70, 112
AVI *125*

AXIS - Visual Arts Information Service 116
Ayers, Alain *27*, 109, 110

B

banners, textile 46, *46*
Bastille Dances 102
BBC Billboard Art Project 23, 34, *34*, 120
Bean, Anne *108*, 109
Bench and light standards *37*
Benyon, Margaret *143*
Between Us 82, *82*
Bews, Phil 97
Biddulph, Jon 54, 134
billboards 34, *34*, *35*, *86*, 120, *125*; *see also* hoardings
Birmingham: Centenary Square *17*, 59; Convention Centre 17, 59; Heartlands 56-7; Holloway Circus underpass 58; 'Honeymoon Project' 102-3, *103*; Jewellery Centre gates *73*; Public Art Commissions Agency 17, 112; St Thomas Peace Gardens 45, *45*, 48, 57
Blum, Andrea 67
body architecture (costumes) 101
bollards, as artform 17, *19*
Boston (USA) 38
Bradford, St Luke's Hospital *92*, 93
Brady, Iain *96*
Braintree, Tabor High School project 48, 132, *132*, 133
brass, as material 73
Brennand Wood, Michael 48, 132, 133
brick, as material 52, 61, *61*, 77
bridges, as sites *69*
Bristol 142; Arnolfini Gallery 44, *101*; Women's Photography Group *86*
British Gas Awards scheme 16, 25
British Health Care Arts 60
British Rail commissions and sites 30, 47, *67*, *69*
British Steel sponsorship 52
Broderick, Richard 51
bronze, as material *67*, *97*, *144*
Brouw, Arthur op den *89*
Brown, Sally *51*
Buckley, John *65*

buildings (houses, industrial etc), as projects/sites *40*, 40-1, *56*, 57, *65*, 103-4, 132, *132*, 133; exteriors used 108, *108*; symbolic functions of artwork in 70; *see also* hospitals
Bull, Steve *121*
Burton, Scott *37*, 37-8
Burwell, Paul 75
businesses *see* corporate sector
Butler, Martyn *108*, 109

C

Camlin, Robert *115*
Canterbury sea benches 80
Cardiff Bay: Arts Trust index 115; landmark *106*
Caring Arts 93
Cartledge, Travey 97
Cascade Amulaire 105
Catrin, Ann *115*
ceilings, as artform *132*
ceramics, as material 57, *76*
Ceravalo, Jan 86
Chadwick, Helen 23, 34, *34*
Chiltern Sculpture Trail *144*
Christo 111
Chrysalis Arts 80, *87*, 87-8, *88*, 101
cibachrome image *137*
Circle 110
The Circular Walk 99
'cities of culture' 16
Cleveland Arts 109-10
Cleveland Way *110*
Clifford, Sue 27
Cocker, Doug 83, *84*, 139
Cole, Richard *13*
collaborations 57, 61, 99, 100, 121; international 102-3; 'invisible' 100, 103-4
Combe Down, Bath 118
comments book, use of 138, 143, 144
commissions 66; applications for 78-9, 83-5, 86, 89, 90-1, 116-17, 128, *129*; artist/commissioner relationship 127-8, 131, 136-7, 140; attributes needed by artist 44-5, 47-8; brief for 91, 92-3, 94-6, 127, and responses to the brief 119-20; budgeting for 84; by corporations 21; consultation, with commissioners and the public 42, 72, 87, 140-4; developing skills 49-51; documented 42, 83, 124; flexibility 57-8; and industry 61; initiated by artists *30*, 78, 79-81, 85, 94, 95, 116, 117-18, *118*; integrated approach to 48, 52; integration 37-8; launching 124-6; mediation between artist, commissioner and public 41-3; negotiation (problem solving) 95, 139-40; presentation by commissioners 128; presentation given by artist 45, 73, 120, 121, 122-4; private 82; production of 46-7; rejection or success 98; relationship between artist and commissioner 127-8, 131, 136-7, 139; structures 79; time-scale for 53-7; work of planners 53; *see also* competitions

Common Ground 26, 27, 110
community: artists working in the 35; residencies in the 22
Community InSight 35
community projects 12, 26, 27, 88, 101, 109-10, 124; budgets 119; rural *141*
companies *see* corporate sector
Company of Imagination *141*, 142
competitions: applying for 85, 89; briefs for 94-5; limited *67*, 79, 142; open 79, 81, 83, 95, 115, 142
compulsory competitive tendering 20, 111
computer-aided designs 47
concrete, as material 50
consultants/artists 19, 22, 48, 50, 78, 82, 127, 131, 132, 133, 136-7
consultation 24, 39-40, 42, 45, 54, 87, 93, 110, 140-141, 142-143
contracts 94, 95, 96, 97
Coppard, Hattie 103
Copper Speakers 120
copyright 90, 116
corporate sector 20-1, 109, 111; sponsorship by 18, 21, 61, 119
courses see training
Coventry Cathedral 104
Cowan, Judith *144*
Crab and Winkle Line 80
'Cuckoo Summit' *26*
Curley, Sean *115*
curriculum vitae 83, 84, 85, 90, 116, 117, 120
cycle paths, as sites *25, 26, 41, 58*

D

Ddart 99
Derelict Land Grants 14-15
Dilworth, Stephen 96
Dine, Jim *20*, 21
disabled artists 138, 142
Docklands Community Project *see* Art of Change
documentation: copyright on 116; of temporary works 124; updating 116; of work 73, 83, 112, 114, 115, 116, 124, 135
Drury, Chris *26*
Duncan of Jordanstone course 49
Dungey, Jan 142

E

Eadon, Jenny *89*
Eastern Arts Board policy 80
East Sussex, 'Cuckoo Summit' *26*
Eaton, Terry 97
Edinburgh 58, 104; Old Calton Cemetery 81; Sculpture Workshop *81*
Employment, Department of, funds 14
engineer/artist collaboration 60
Environment, Department of the 14, 65
environmental issues (conservation) 24, 26, *26*, 71; *see also* recycled materials
environment and art 48, 51, *97, 141*

Essex County Council 84
Evans, Alan 47
Everybody's World AIDS Day 72
exhibitions: documentation of 114; open-air sculpture 22; 'Tyne International' 56

F

Farrell, Michael 50
Farringdon, Richard *110*
Faulkner, Rick 80, 86, 95, 111
fellowships 84
Ferrara, Jackie 38
Festival Bridges 69
Festival of Britain (1951) 14, 104
Fête 31
fibreglass, as material *96*
Fine Rats International 75, 77
Fink, Peter *108*, 109, 141-2
Fisher, Karl 50
Fleming, Martha *40*, 40-1
Flock 84
flooring, as artform 59, 69, 97, 130, *132*
Flow City 32
Flying Costumes, Floating Tombs 101
Forbury Lion 89
Forestry Commission 144
Form and Function project 33
Forster, John *121*
Foster-Ogg, Simon 80
France: Beaux Arts System 103; Bicentenary *102*; collaborative projects 105-6; consultant/artist 131
Fraser, Ian 132, 133
Freeform Arts Trust 51
Fuller, Mark 80
funding 11; Arts Council 15-16; by the corporate sector 20-1; by government 12, 13, 14; by local authorities 17-18; by South West Arts 80; fundraising for a project 118-19, 136; for training 50
furniture, as artform *22*

G

Gant, Lynne 83
garden festivals *14*, 14-15, 25, 48, 52, *69*
Garden Festival Wales 48, 52, *52*, *59*, 61, *61*
Garden of Hope 50
gardens, as sites 51, 53, 71; community 50; mosaic 56
gates, as artform 47, 50, *73*
Gateshead *13*, *56*, 57; Garden Festival *14*, 15, 25, 56, *69*, 82
Gec, Stefan 35-7, *36*
Gerz, Jochen and Esther 39, *39*
Glanfield, William 80
Glasgow 15, 25; City of Culture 44, 52; Garnethill 52; 'Keeping Glasgow in Stitches' project 46; School of Art 49
glass, as material 57, 73
Glory of the Garden policy 15-16

Gloucester, Eastgate Shopping Centre *121*
Goldsworthy, Andy *41*
Gomila, Francis *75*, *106*
Gorvin, Diane 97
government: funding 12-15; local 12, 32; *see also* local authorities
graduates, work experience for 51
Griffiths, Stuart *115*
de Groot, Dennis 99-100
Gustafson, Kathryn 53, *53*, 56

H

Harris, Richard *24*
Haselden, Ron *30*, *31*, 31
Hatton, Peter 101, 134
Have Your Cake and Eat It 137
Head for the Hills 124
Heathfield/Polegate, Sustrans cycle path 26
Heeney, Gwen *61*, 61
Herbe Garden 71
Heslop, Maura 48
Hilton Parish Council 110
hoardings 35, 136; *see also* billboards
Hobbins, Nigel 80
Hodgson, Janet 101
holograms *143*
Holzer, Jenny *36*
Homeless Projections 38
Homeless Vehicle 38, *38*
Home Office, funds 14
'Honeymoon Project' 102-3
Hooky 79
'House Project' 56, 57
hospitals, as sites 11, *60*, 83, *92*, 93, 123, *124*, *137*, Special Care Baby Unit 138, *138*
Hunter, Ian *115*

I

Ikon Gallery 102, 103
Incentive Funding Scheme 15, 21
industrial sites *13*, 15, *41*, *59*
installations 29-31, *108*, *117*, *121*
insurance (and professional indemnity) 90, 105, 111
International Women's Festival 86
interviews 120-2, 124
Investment in the Future of Fine Art in Public Places survey 49-50
Ipswich 'Arts in Town' project *71*; Christchurch Park *71*
Irwin, Robert *68*, 75-6, 77

J

Jagonari Mosaic 70
Jagonari Women's Centre 70
Janvanj banner 46, *46*
Jaray, Tess *17*, 59-60
Johnson, Michael *73*
Journey 97
Jump Fucker Jump 75

K

Karmardin, Anatoly *76*
Kaur, Permindar *120*
Kelly, Jane 103, 128, 129, *129*, 133, 136, 137
Khan, Keith 101
Kiehlmann, Sandi 46, *46*
Koenig, Robert *122*
Kozloff, Joyce 67

L

La Donna Delinquenta 40
lamp-posts, as artform 17, 37
landmarks, as artform *106, 142*
landscape designers/architects 51, 52, 57, 59, 61, 105
landscape projects *68, 71*
landscape sculpture 15, 41, 53, 56, 59
Langslie Spiral 57, *58*
language (iconography) of artists 33-7
Lapointe, Lyne *40*, 40-1
lasers, as medium 108, *108*, 109
Layered Lattices 123
Leeson, Loraine *35*, 50
Leicester 47; Newarke underpass 47- 8, 60
letter boxes, as artform 96
Lewisham, 2000 team *19*, 131
light display, as artform 30, 31, *75*, 97, 108;
　　advertising board 72; shopping centre installation
　　121
Light Wave 30, 30-1
Light Year 108
Living Space 134, 134-5, *135*
local authorities 12, 14, 16, 17-20, 47, 54, 58, 59, 118;
　　percent for art policies 32
London Broadgate development *20*, 21, 29, 101, 104;
　　Canary Wharf 31, 108, *108*, 109; Docklands 109;
　　Greenwich/Thames Barrier *117*; Hammersmith
　　Hospital 123, 138; Leicester Square Underground
　　Station *36*; Oxford Circus poster 125; Piccadilly
　　Circus *72*; St George's Hospital *60*; West London
　　Hospital *137*; Wimbledon Station and town hall *67*
Loophole Cinema 75

M

McHugh, Christopher 72
McLean, Bruce 106, 107
Maddison, Kate 80, 101
Magnus, Dieter 52
Mahenthiralingam, Usha *92*
Maiden Outdoor Advertising 72
Maine, John *19*, 131
Manchester 54; Piccadilly Station 97; Royal Infirmary
　　124; Upper Campfield Market *134*, 134-5
Manpower Services Commission (MSC) *13*, 14, 18
maquettes *see* models/maquettes
Margam Sculpture Park 48
Maria, Walter de 29
Marks and Spencer 115
The Masham Leaves 27
Mason, Paul *74*

Maze 41
media coverage 108, 122, 125-6, 135
mediation 41-42, 44-45, 51
Meeting Point 53
memorials 82, *82, 140*
metalwork 47, 48, 50-1, 73; *see also* wrought iron
Metropolis 122, 126
Miller, Roland 75, 131
Milner, Liz 86
Miralda, Antoni 102, 103
Miss, Mary 35, 38, 67, *68*
models/maquettes 91, 94, 143
Moncur, Jennie 69
Monument against Fascism 39, 39-40
Moore, Graeme *71*
Moore, Nick 118, *118*, 119
mosaic 60, *70*, 88; garden 56; murals 47, *47, 124*
Mother Earth 59
murals 47, *47,* 51, *70, 124*
Murray, Val 134, 139, 141

N

National Artists Register 116
National Health Service 14
Neal, Jenni 50-1
Nechells Library commission 45
Newcastle, High Level Bridge 35-7
New Dolphin Mooring Post 51
'New Forms in Willow' 24, 26
'New Milestones' projects 26, 27, *27*, 110, *110*
New York 38, *40*, 42; artist-in- residence in Dept of
　　Sanitation 32; Battery Park 21, *22, 68*; Foley
　　Square *23*, 23-4; Museum of Holography 143
'Niches Project' *81*
9 Spaces 9 Trees 68
nocturnal events 75
Norse Longship 141
Northampton, Guildhall Extension commission *74*
Northern Arts Board policy 80
North Shields, Fish Quay *51*
Northumberland, Ashington Leisure Centre *79*
North West Arts policy 80
The Nottingham Sculpture 30, 31

O

Oak under Oak 48
Obelisk 52, *52*
Oberon, Peat 50-1
Oxford Sculpture Project 144

P

PACA *see* Public Art Commissions Agency
pageants 101, 141
Pages of the Diary 76
'parachute art' 11, 23, 26
Parc Glynllifon, Wales *115*
Paris, Parc de la Villette Science Museum *105*
Parkin, Andy 72
parks, as sites 15, *37*, 71, 87, 105, 115, 135
Partnership Arts 54, 55, 97

partnerships 16, 18
Partridge, Jim *25, 50,* 51
Patel, Anu *45,* 45-6, 48, 56
Patten, David 128, 129, *129,* 133, 136
paving schemes and pavements *17, 66,* 77, 97
Peace Gardens *see* Birmingham
Pearce, Colin 75
The Pearl of the Gulf 105, *105*
Pemberton, Jan 86
Penzance 82
percent for art 16, 17, 18, 21, 32, 104; in America 66
performance art 75, 99-100, *101*
Perry, Richard *74*
Petts, Mick 59
Phaophanit, Vong *117*
Philadelphia 33
photography: as artform *60*; photo-copied *86*; photo-mural *35*; as documentation 124; for temporary works 38
photo-montage 94, *106*
Pilling, Lynn 134
Piper Alpha Memorial 140
planners 19-20
playgrounds 51
Plouër-sur-Rance *31*
Plymouth 55
poem, in cast concrete 50
Poesis Generator 106
porch, as artform *56*
portfolios of work 83, 91
posts, as artform *19,* 87
Pragnell, Valerie 48, 57, *58*
Pratz, Guihelm 106
presentation of work: at an interview (formal or informal) 122, 123, 124; for a commission 73, 121, 123
press releases 125
Projects Environment 24, 26
proposals for a project 78-9, 85, 87-8, 89-90; for 'projects not yet realised' 83
Pryke, Nick 132
PT119 36
Public Art Commissions Agency (PACA) 17, 44, 45, 48, 57, 103, 112
Public Art Consultancy Team 11
Public Art Development Trust 47, 112, 117, 132, 138
Public Art Forum 18
Public Arts 30, 59

Q

Quarryman 118, *118*
Quick, Charles *30,* 30-1
Quick, Sarah *86*

R

railings *45,* 50-1
Reading Visual Arts Week *89*
recycled materials 13, 25, 32
Red Army 14

Redditch, Spastics Society office *142,* 142-3
Red Herring Studios 72
regional arts associations (RAA) 16, 18; arts funding 14; slide registers 115-16
regional arts boards: award schemes 119; information leaflets 80; one-to-one surgeries to discuss projects 85; slide indexes and registers 115-16
registers: for disabled artists 142; for slides 83, 112, 115-16, 117
Renn, Mark 50, 75
residencies 22, 24, 46, 78, 79, 127, 141; at hospital 138; in government departments 32; information on 80; in schools 57
Reynolds, Adam *142,* 142-3
Rice, Peter 106
Ridge, Sue 44, *47,* 47-8, 57-8, 60, 62
Ring 102-3, *103*
Ritchie, Ian *105,* 105-6, *106*
Roberts, Jim *51*
Robinson, Graham 51
Robinson, Susanna 63-4, 83
Ross, Christopher *79*
Russell, Kate 78, 79, 144

S

Sainsbury, J, commission for 54-5
sanitation department, artist's work with 32-3
schools 78; projects involving 26, 57, 81, 101; residencies in 57; as site 11
Scotland: Countryside Commission 141; Local Enterprise Councils 14
Scullion, Louise 96
sculpture trails 57, 96, *144*
seating (benches), as artform 17, *25, 37,* 50, *50,* 51, 55, *80*; as a memorial 82, *82*
Seattle: Arts Commission 72-3; Public Safety Building Plaza *68*
Segal, George 21
self-employment 50
Serra, Richard 21, 23, *23,* 42
Shadows of the Past 82
Shark 65, *65*
Sheffield: Campus 21 (City Polytechnic) 128, 129, 136; Don Valley Stadium *66*; Pond Street area 129; Tudor Square *74*
Shell 53
Short, Denys 52, *52, 115*
Sitting/Stance 22
Skelton and Brotton Milestones 110
slag pile, as site 59
slides: for an application 117, 120; how to take them 113-14; libraries 112, 115; as presentation of work 90, 91, 112; registers and indexes 83, 112, 115-16, 117; updating them 116
Smith, Ivan 75
Smith, Ray *14*
Smithson, Robert 29
Solar Markers 143
son et lumière *31*

Southampton Station 47, *47*
South Cove 68
South West Arts policy 80
Spiral Jetty 29
sponsorship 11, 47, 86, 118, 119; by companies *14*, 21, 61; by local companies 18
START community arts project *124*
Station House Opera 102
steel: as material *23*, 47, 82, 129; stainless 52, *52*, 73
Stockton Riverside Festival 101
Stoke Museum and Art Gallery 134, *135*
stone, as medium 13, 50, 51, *74, 80,* 109-10, 129
Stone, Paul *137*
Stormer, — *107*
Stornaway, An Lanntair Arts Centre 96
Strategy for Public Art in Cardiff Bay 11, 22
Strathclyde, Sculpture Trail 57
street furniture *17, 19, 37,* 38
streets 51
Sunderland: St Peter's Riverside Sculpture Project 50, 82; Training Agency 51
Sustrans 25, 26, 41, 57, 58
subversion, as a working method 99-100, *125*

T

Tabor School *see* Braintree
Tacha, Athena 67
Taylor, Sue Jane *140*
teamwork 51, 59-60, 61, 62, 72, 105-7
Tebby, Susan *123*
temporary works 38-41, *74,* 100, 101, 108, *108,* 109, *125,* 135; documentation of 124; funding for 16
textiles 57, 69, *92,* 93; *see also* banners
Thakor, Meena 70
Those Environmental Artists *134,* 134-5,
Tilted Arc 23, *23,* 42
Touching Earth and Sky 144
town artists 78
Trace Elements 35-7, 36
Trade and Industry, Department of 14
Trafford 54; Davyhulme Park *87,* 87- 8, *88*
trails *see* animated trails; sculpture trails
training 14, 49-51, 65-6, 78, 141; lack of 64, 104
Training and Enterprise Councils 14, 50
Tree 74
tree grilles *74*
TSWA 'Four Cities' project 23, 35, 117

U

Ukeles, Mierle 32-3
undergraduates, placements for 51
United States of America policies and attitudes 31-2, 66-7, 70, 77
Urban Development Corporations 12-13, 14, 18
Urban Programme 12, 15, 16

V

Vandalism 24, 39
Veevers, Joanna *66*
Venus 20

video: used in presentation of work 90, 91, 94, 123; used in projects 32-3, 75
village, sculpture project in 109-10
Viner, Darrell 117

W

Wakefield 142; Cathedral Precinct 59-60; Public Arts 86; Station *30,* 30-1
Wales: Countryside Council for 50; literature projects *115*; University of *50; see also* Garden Festival Wales
Walking Women 67
Wallace, Andre *67*
walling, drystone 57
Walmsley, Liz 25, 50
water displays/features, as artform 53, 57, *58*, 101, 123, *123,* 129
Watkins, David 48
Waygood, Jem 54
Welsh Arts Council Slide Registry 115
West meets East 35
What falls to the ground, but can't be eaten 117
What goes down must come up! 79
Whitstable Artists and Musicians collective 80
Wilbourn, Colin 50, 82, *82*
The Wilds and the Deep 40
Williams, Bruce 72
Williams, Catrin *115*
Willis, Nancy 138, *138*
Willow Walk 24
Wills, Alison 86
Winchester School of Art course 49
Winds of Change 54-5, *55*
Windy Nook 13
Wodiczko, Krzysztof 38, *38*
Wolverhampton Station commission 46-7
women artists 112, 133
Women Artists Slide Library 112
Women of Colour Slide Index 112
wood, as material *25, 26,* 48, 50, *50,* 51, *80,* 82, *84,* 132
Woof, Paula 46-7, 54, 57
Woolhouse, Sue *51*
Working for Cities Awards 16, 21, 25
working methods *see* collaborations; subversion; teamwork
workshops 24
Wreath to Pleasure 34
Wright, Georgia *80*
Wright, Terry *60*
wrought iron 57
Wyllie, George 96

Y

Yorkshire and Humberside Arts Board policy 80

Essential reading for artists, makers & photographers

"The best and most consistent series [of] publications... cannot be praised too highly."
Marina Vaizey

"AN Publications' paperback series provides practical advice and information to help artists of all kinds."
Sam Yates, Crafts Council Bookshop

"AN Publications are in the business of producing really excellent guides to the... business of being an artist and staying above water."
Robin Stemp, The Artist

AN Publications produces a whole range of publications on the visual arts. They can be bought from good bookshops, or by mail order from us. Many are listed below, but for further information or an up-to-date catalogue, please contact us at

PO Box 23, Sunderland, SR4 6DG, 091 514 3600, fax 091 564 1600.
(Please add 10% to prices to cover postage unless you subscribe to *Artists Newsletter* in which case postage is free.)

*Prices quoted are the prices in force as of October 1992 and are subject to change.

"...without a doubt the most useful and informative artists' magazine in Britain today."

artists newsletter

"Artists Newsletter has been a lifeline to me and I'm sure it is to other people."

The essential monthly read for everyone working in the visual arts. Packed to the gills with up-to-the-minute information, it is a vital resource for all artists, makers, photographers, and administrators.

Artists Newsletter features:

■ **Comprehensive listings of awards, commissions, open exhibitions, residencies, competitions and other opportunities for artists**

■ **Regular articles on artistic and professional practice**

■ **Help, Letters and News pages**

■ **Exhibition and live art listings**

■ **A highly popular small ads section**

Subscribe and get:
12 issues for less than the price of 9! Plus free early delivery to your door.
Ask for a FREE sample issue.

Individual subscriptions:
£16 UK, £24 Eire/Europe, £30 other (air)
Institute subscriptions:
£28 UK, £38 Eire/Europe, £50 other (air)

Fact Packs

Indispensible factsheets for artists, makers and administrators. Buy any 3 and save money!

■ **Craft Fairs**
Includes a selected list of national and international fairs with details.

■ **Getting TV & Radio Coverage**
Includes a contact list of TV and radio stations.

■ **Green Art Materials**
Includes a listing of suppliers of 'green' products.

■ **Insurance**
Advice on the types of insurance artists need, and why.

■ **Mailing the Press**
Includes a press list of national dailies, weeklies and magazines.

■ **Postgraduate Courses**
Includes a listing of courses.

■ **Rates of Pay**
Updated information on current pay rates for artists.

■ **Slide Indexes**
Includes a national listing of artists' registers and slide indexes.

■ **Buying Clay, Buying a Kiln**
A comprehensive listing of suppliers and manufacturers in the UK.

■ **Travelling, Working & Selling in the EC**
Current regulations, sources of funding and lists of contacts.

■ **New Technology for the Visual Arts**
Sources of information on facilities, training, equipment and suppliers.

Single Fact Packs **£1.85 UK, £2.25 Eire/Europe, £3 other (air)**
Any 3 Fact Packs **£4.50 UK, £5.10 Eire/Europe, £6.25 other (air)**

Directory of Exhibition Spaces 93/94

(3rd edition) ed Richard Padwick

"No self-respecting artist who wants to show and sell work should be without it."
　　Working for Yourself in the Arts and Crafts

A comprehensive listing of over 2000 galleries in the UK and Eire to help you find the right exhibition space. Details who to apply to, type of work shown, space and facilities. An unrivalled visual arts reference resource with an impressive track record, now published biennially

256 pages, illustrated £13.99

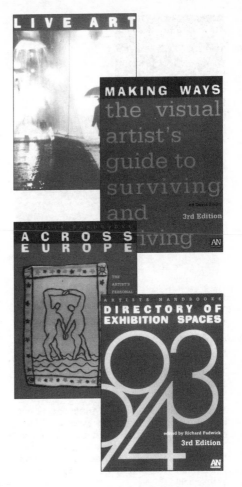

Across Europe:

the artist's personal guide to travel and work
ed David Butler

"... a much needed sourcebook."
　　Sam Yates, Crafts Council Bookshop

A combination of artists' first-hand experiences and hard facts gets under the Eurospeak to show what '1992-and-all-that' could mean for you. Over 20 European nations are covered, giving information on: organisations, funding, magazines, agencies and other sources of information. A must for everyone interested in selling, exhibiting, working or training in Europe.

168 pages, illustrated £9.95

Making Ways:

the artist's guide to surviving and thriving
3rd edition, ed David Butler

"...a thorough and thoughtful compilation of fact, theory and practicle example... a vital part of every visual and applied artist's survival kit."　　Gail Boardman, Craftwork

New edition of the visual artist's professional bible, revised and brought bang up-to-date to help you 'survive and thrive' in the '90s. Features important new sections on selling, presentation and opportunities abroad. Everything you need to know about the 'business end' of being an artist.

288 pages, illustrated £11.99

Live Art

ed Robert Ayers & David Butler　　*"an inspiration"* Live Art Listings

What is live art? How far does it overlap and integrate with other art forms? However you define your art, if it involves live or non-permanent elements this book is for you. It includes advice on putting a performance together, touring work, copyright, contracts and documentation, with examples of live art through photographs and comments by artists. For everyone who wants to develop, earn from, or promote live art.

178 pages, illustrated £9.95

Health & Safety:
making art &
avoiding dangers
Tim Challis & Gary Roberts

"It is in the interest of all artists to study the contents of this handbook."
Leisure Painter

Making art can be dangerous. Artists and makers now use substances and processes which can damage human health and the environment. This unique handbook covers all art and craft forms to help you protect people and the environment, and prepare your COSHH assessment.

144 pages, illustrated £7.25

Copyright:
protection, use &
responsibilities
Roland Miller

"...a comprehensive guide."
Portfolio Magazine

Essential advice on negotiating rewarding copyright agreements; exploiting the earning and promotional potential of copyright; and dealing with infringement of copyright. Designed to help *you* make the most of copyright.

128 pages, illustrated £7.25

Organising Your Exhibition:
the self-help guide
Debbie Duffin

"A do-it-yourself guide designed to help... artists to get their work on the wall with the minimum of agony."
Wideangle

"...detailed advice on pitfalls ranging from dealing with printers to buying wine."
Art Monthly

The revised and updated edition of Debbie Duffin's invaluable practical guide offers excellent advice on finding space, finances, publicity, insurance, framing and hanging work, private views, and selling. The essential sourcebook on setting up and running any exhibition.

116 pages £7.25

Money Matters:
the artist's financial guide
Sarah Deeks, Richard Murphy & Sally Nolan

"...recommended".
Ceramic Review

Reliable user-friendly advice on: tax, National Insurance, VAT, keeping accounts, pricing your work, grants, insurance, dealing with customers, suppliers and banks, and much more. Features an accounting system specially devised for artists.

134 pages, illustrated £7.25